THE GREAT
MARGARITA
BOOK

THE GREAT
MARGARITA
BOOK

AL LUCERO

WITH JOHN HARRISSON

TEN SPEED PRESS
BERKELEY, CALIFORNIA

1☉ TEN SPEED PRESS
P.O. BOX 7123
BERKELEY, CA 94707
WWW.TENSPEED.COM

DISTRIBUTED IN AUSTRALIA BY SIMON AND SCHUSTER
AUSTRALIA, IN CANADA BY TEN SPEED PRESS CANADA, IN
NEW ZEALAND BY SOUTHERN PUBLISHERS GROUP, IN
SOUTH AFRICA BY REAL BOOKS, IN SOUTHEAST ASIA BY
BERKELEY BOOKS, AND IN THE UNITED KINGDOM AND
EUROPE BY AIRLIFT BOOK COMPANY.

COVER DESIGN BY GARY BERNAL
TEXT DESIGN BY CHRIS HALL BASED ON A DESIGN
BY GARY BERNAL

PHOTOGRAPHS BY SCOTT VLAUN

LIBRARY OF CONGRESS CATALOGING-IN-PUBLICATION DATA
ON FILE WITH THE PUBLISHER.

ISBN 1-58008-053-7
FIRST PRINTING, 1999

PRINTED IN CHINA

7 8 9 10 — 04 03

Contents

FOREWORD

There was a time when a state of mind could be defined or cured by a good martini. It was a benchmark for a good time, a good lunch, a good date, a great place. The Great American Drink.

No more. Now, more often than not, in more places than most, that American measuring stick has given way to the new king: The Margarita. I don't know where or when or even how this started. I just know it's here. So now we hear about restaurants or bars defined by how great their margaritas are.

What constitutes a truly great margarita is not that easy to define. It is at once elusive and unforgiving. I once had a margarita in Westport, Connecticut, and threw up an hour later. I've had margaritas that were watered down, over-sweetened, too sour, and some strange color. (Can there be a good strawberry margarita?) One thing is certain. When you have a real margarita, you know it.

When people have asked of a place to eat in Santa Fe, I find myself referring them to Maria's. Is it fancy? No. Is it chic? No. Is the food good? Yes. But the margaritas—they are the best. When you read this book, you'll know why. Like anything of quality, it takes love and care—a degree of passion to execute it, love to start it, commitment to that love to sustain it. Maria's is a history and a definition. I am glad it's there. I'm glad I've tasted their margaritas, and I hope not too many people find out about it.

Robert Redford

INTRODUCTION

I can remember first seeing the Maria's sign out front of the adobe-style building when I was about 14 or 15 years old, back in the early fifties. I was born and raised in Santa Fe, New Mexico, and back then a new restaurant was big news. The only others I can remember are the Pink Adobe, The Pantry, the El Gancho on the old Las Vegas Highway (now Old Pecos Trail), and a truck stop out on old Highway 85 (C errillos Road). Of course there was the La Fonda Hotel (a Santa Fe landmark), and I knew there was a "ritzy" restaurant inside, but it was only for adults and tourists with lots of money.

The state had just moved the old New Mexico state penitentiary south of town (having razed the old pen, which was located catty-corner to Maria's). Little did I imagine that the original owners of Maria's would be buying the used brick from the demolition of the pen to decorate the inside of a restaurant that, 30 years later, I would own.

Maria's is not just a historic Santa Fe landmark; it almost qualifies as a museum. The beer cooler is a converted icebox dating back to the 1880s that was shipped in from its perch in the old gold rush town of Dawson in northern New Mexico. (My dad was a six-gun-toting deputy U.S. marshal in the area of Dawson at the turn of the century, so he could have easily had a couple of beers from that very icebox while it was still in its original spot.) The hand-carved and painted beams in the east room come from the old Public Service Company building in downtown Santa Fe. Much of the furniture throughout the restaurant is from the pre–World War II La Fonda Hotel. And the famous Santa Fe artist Alfred Morang painted wall frescoes in the cantina in exchange for food and drink. (We had these priceless paintings restored by local restoration experts who relished the job because of their admiration for Morang. Now the work of dozens of other Santa Fe artists hangs on the walls of Maria's as well.)

The Maria's tradition began in 1952 when Maria Lopez and her husband, Gilbert, started a take-out kitchen on the very same spot, in the very same building where Maria's exists today. As business boomed for the young Lopez couple, they slowly expanded, adding two booths and a patio.

Over the years, Maria's had its ups and downs. My wife Laurie and I are the fifth owners of Maria's. After moving back to Santa Fe following my career as a television executive (which took us all over the country), Laurie and I, like a lot of other couples, used to dine out a lot. We would critique each restaurant we visited and tell each other how we could have made it better. Relying on this great store of knowledge, we bought Maria's on December 1, 1985. We had history on our side: I am an umpteenth-generation descendant of one of the old Spanish conquistadors who captained an army that occupied Santa Fe in the seventeenth century—so my family has been cooking and eating New Mexican food for centuries.

Before we moved back to Santa Fe, we had been looking forward to enjoying the wonderful New Mexican cooking at local restaurants. Unfortunately, once we got there we were disappointed. Some things had changed since I was a kid. Soupy beans and posole were being served on the plate with no broth. Tacos were being filled with roast beef and potatoes. Tortillas were all machine made. Margaritas were being poured out of slush-type machines. I had been making margaritas in a blender, using sweetened, frozen lime juice as far back as the 1960s. I can remember adding sugar to give the slush some flavor. Shortly after buying Maria's, I discovered that making margaritas with lime or lemon juice, triple sec, and tequila shaken with ice brought out the flavors of the ingredients. That was when I started experimenting with various tequilas. When we bought Maria's, we decided we were going to do things right. And we did. We served beans and posole in a bowl with broth, we made our tortillas by hand, and we introduced properly served fajitas to Santa Fe—which of course had to be accompanied by margaritas!

Having researched other aspects of our restaurant to make sure that it was as authentic as possible, we were determined to make the best margarita anywhere in the world! We studied up on tequila in Mexico and emphasized the quality and flavor of 100-percent agave tequila, mixing it with freshly squeezed lemon juice and naturally flavored triple sec, rather than manufactured sugar-sweetened drink mixes. We were amazed what a difference it made to use only the best-quality ingredients.

Our attention to detail and our determination to make the best and purest margaritas possible have paid off. The *New York Times* called Maria's margaritas the "best in town." The *Washington Post* said they are "world class." *Southern Arts* described Maria's as "Margaritaville" and named our margaritas as one of the 101 reasons to visit Santa Fe. The *Seattle*

Times described us as "the mother lode of American margaritas." From *Better Homes and Gardens* to *Playboy*, newspapers and magazines nationwide, as well as almost every state and local publication, have given our margaritas rave reviews.

Most Americans are used to drinking poor or mediocre tequila, whether straight or in a margarita. The purpose of this book is to share the knowledge of how to recognize and appreciate a good tequila, and how to make the purest, most delightful cocktail on earth: a great margarita!

¡Salud!

Al Lucero

CHAPTER ONE

TEQUILA
The Soul of a
Real Margarita

You want a great margarita, right? Then it makes sense that you should use only the best ingredients to make it, especially when it comes to tequila. At Maria's in Santa Fe, we call our great margaritas "real margaritas" because we use only real ingredients: real tequila, real triple sec, and real lemon or lime juice. However, just because a bottle has the word "tequila" on its label does not automatically mean that it contains real tequila. So it's important to learn the basic facts about tequila.

Tequila is an 80-proof liquor (40 percent alcohol by volume) that is made only in Mexico. It is double-distilled from the sugary juices extracted from the cooked piña, or heart, of the blue agave plant (botanically named *Agave tequilana Weber*, blue variety). Although there are 360 varieties of agave, the blue agave is the only one from which tequila can be made.

By the early 1990s, tequila had become the tenth best-selling spirit in the United States (vodka is the market leader). The United States not only imports more tequila than any other country in the world, but it also consumes more tequila than Mexico. Tequila is also the fastest-growing spirit in terms of sales, largely because of the ever-increasing popularity of margaritas.

The Mexican government maintains strict control over the production of tequila and imposes exacting regulations on its distillers, the most important of which mandates that all tequila must be distilled twice and must contain at least 51 percent blue agave sugar. Any product with less than 51 percent blue agave sugar cannot, by the Mexican government's standards, be considered tequila. So from now on we'll call tequila with 51 percent or more agave sugar "real" tequila and that with less than 51 percent agave sugar "unreal."

The agave sugars used in making tequila can best be described by comparing the manufacturing of tequila to the making of maple syrup. If one were to take the sap of a maple tree and mix it with corn syrup, it would not be pure maple syrup; it would be syrup with natural maple flavoring. Obviously, the higher the percentage of pure maple sap (sugar) used to make the syrup, the better the maple flavor that would result. The same chemistry applies to tequila. The higher the percentage of agave sugar used to make the tequila, the better the quality of the tequila. If the tequila is made with less than 100 percent agave sugar, cane sugar dissolved in distilled water is added.

In addition to regulating the percentage of agave sugar, the Mexican government also requires that the agave plants used to make real tequila can only be grown in one of five Mexican states: Jalisco, Michoacán, Nayarit, Tamaulipas, or Guanajuato. Like fine Burgundy wines grown in different microclimates of adjacent valleys and mountain sides, there is a distinctive difference in flavor between tequilas (such as El Tesoro and Centinela) grown in the highlands of Jalisco around Arandas, and those (like José Cuervo) grown in the foothills near the village of Tequila, which is still the center of the tequila industry.

After the required 51 percent blue agave sugar, the remaining 49 percent (or less) of the liquid in tequila is generally water with cane sugar (usually Mexican-grown) which is added to the blue agave sugar during fermentation. Some tequilas contain much more than the required 51 percent blue agave; however, only those tequilas that are 100 percent blue agave are required to list this percentage on the label. It is also required that each bottle of tequila (whether bottled in Mexico or elsewhere) carry the distiller's NOM (*Norma Oficial Mexicana*, or "official Mexican standard") number. This four-digit-plus-one-letter number is issued only to tequila distillers who can consistently pass government inspections and comply with the required regulations for the production of tequila. If a bottle of tequila does not have the distiller's NOM number on the label, it is not real tequila, even if the label says "Made in Mexico."

To appreciate premium tequila fully, it is important to understand that there are significant differences between premium tequila that merely complies with the Mexican government's minimum requirement of 51 percent blue agave and the best-quality superpremium tequila distilled from 100 percent blue agave juice (known as *miel* in Mexico) with nothing else added.

All 100-percent blue agave tequilas must be bottled in Mexico and can only be exported in their original bottles. On the other hand, other tequilas can be and usually are exported in railroad tank cars or tanker trucks and then bottled at plants in various cities, usually in the United States.

Both premium and superpremium tequilas come in several different grades. Here is where it gets interesting: different grades of tequila result in different kinds of margaritas. The different types of tequila are categorized as *plata* or *blanco* ("silver" or "white" tequila); gold, also called *joven abocado* ("young and smoothed"); *reposado* ("rested," or aged for a brief time); *añejo* ("aged"); and *muy añejo* ("very aged").

Plata is freshly fermented and double-distilled tequila, which is usually bottled or shipped immediately after distillation. Premium plata tequila, like all other premium tequilas, is bottled in Mexico and shipped in the bottle. Plata is the most commonly produced of all tequilas. I personally enjoy premium plata tequila more than any other, whether for sipping or for my favorite cocktail, a great margarita.

Gold (or joven abocado) tequila (are you ready to have your lifelong Jimmy Buffett image of tequila destroyed?) is generally freshly distilled plata with caramel food coloring added to darken its appearance and give it an attractive golden hue. The Spanish word for gold, *oro*, actually is very seldom used in describing tequila, rather, añejo or muy añejo is used. Aged tequilas may be gold in color also, but the color is the result of the process of aging in oak barrels (the longer it's aged in oak, the darker the color).

Reposado tequila is carefully aged in oak barrels for a minimum of 2 months and for no longer than 1 year. The color of the tequila will take on a little of the oaken tint from the wooden barrel, but sometimes the difference between plata tequila and reposado is almost indistinguishable. The "resting" process enhances the flavor of reposado and may make the tequila a bit more mellow, but it does not really affect the flavor of a margarita. Most reposado tequilas are superpremium 100-percent agave tequilas.

Añejo tequila has been aged in oak barrels for a minimum of 1 year, a process that must be certified by the Mexican government. The color of añejo tequila varies, but most often it is a soft golden hue, not the deep gold of artificially colored "gold" tequilas. Almost all añejo and muy añejo tequilas are superpremium tequilas.

Muy añejo tequila is aged in oak barrels for more than 2 years and, as with añejo tequila, the aging process must be certified by the Mexican government. Unlike whisky, tequila does not age well over long periods of time. As a matter of fact, tequila will reach its peak in oak in 2 to 4 years. If left on oak for 5 or 6 years, tequila is almost always "turned" (spoiled)—much like bottled wine that has not been properly stored. However, once bottled, tequila will keep as well as most other distilled spirits; and like other spirits, it finishes aging once it's removed from the oak barrels. The color of muy añejo tequila is naturally darker than the añejo, because it has been exposed to the oak wood longer; its coloring comes from the oak. Like a fine cognac, muy añejo is wonderful for sipping, and it also creates a distinctive taste treat when used in a margarita.

Two other Mexican liquors, mezcal and pulque, are sometimes confused with tequila. The one that sometimes has a worm in the bottle is mezcal (the worm inside a mezcal bottle is actually the parasitic moth larva that eats the roots of the agave plant). Mezcal is generally made from the blue agave, but it can also be made from other types of agave. Mezcal may be processed and distilled differently and unlike tequila, mezcal is not inspected or regulated by the Mexican government. There are some wonderful mezcals, but some can be more like American moonshine, so be careful!

Pulque (pronounced "pool-kae") could very easily be called the grandfather of tequila. It is the awful-tasting, undistilled fermented juice of the agave. Legend has it that centuries before the Spanish came to Mexico, lightning lit a wild agave plant on fire, cooking the piña and leaving its juices to ferment into a strong alcoholic liquid. The ancient Mexican Indians drank this liquid and, as a result, had great hallucinations that they reported to their priests. The priests then tried the vino agave, believed it allowed them to communicate with the gods, and proceeded to use the beverage for medicinal and religious purposes. The Spanish arrived and realized that the bitter juice was stronger than the wine they had brought with them; in an attempt to improve the flavor, they distilled it—not once but twice. Hence, eventually, tequila. To this day, pulque is still sold and imbibed in Mexico, although most of it is not actually made from the highly coveted blue agave plant. There is no government control of pulque—so again, be careful!

As with fine wines, whiskies, or brandies (and a lot else besides), with tequila, you get what you pay for. You pay more for better quality. This means that 100-percent blue agave tequilas are more expensive. But, not to worry. You don't need superpremium tequila to make a great margarita. After all, who can afford to have Chateau Margaux or Opus One with dinner every night? Don't count on using 100-percent agave tequila every time you have a margarita. Close to half of the margaritas in this book, including Maria's Special, our house margarita, use premium tequila. If you follow our recipes, you won't be disappointed.

Whose Tequila Is It Anyway?

The saying goes that tequila was discovered by the people of Mexico hundreds of years ago, but it was only discovered by Americans in the 1990s! Oh, tequila has been trickling into the United States for a long time, ever since José Cuervo delivered the first batch to New Mexico back at the turn of the century. Herradura was the first 100-percent agave super premium tequila to be imported into the United States, and it still has a well-established base of sales that is hard to discount. But in the late 1980s and early 1990s, there were two Americans who set the ball rolling for the U.S. tequila marketing boom: Bob Denton and Martin Crowley.

Bob Denton perhaps has influenced the superpremium tequila importing industry more than anyone else in the country. Denton, together with his partner Marilyn Smith, had a good deal of success importing and marketing Chinaco tequila back in the 1980s—it achieved cult status and was a favorite of rock stars, among others. Bob was sailing along selling all the Chinaco his Mexican associates could produce when the bottom fell out! The Chinaco plant in Mexico closed down; rumors vary as to the reason, ranging from a family fight for control to the more colorful story that Mexican mobsters had shut it down by destroying the distillery and hijacking truckloads of the finished product.

Regardless, there was no more Chinaco coming into the United States; the little that was left was warehoused by Denton or was on dealers' shelves (mostly in California). Why is human nature such that when we *can't* have something, we *must* have it? Such was the case with Chinaco tequila. Everyone wanted Chinaco. The price went through the ceiling. If Chinaco had been a cult thing earlier, it became a legend now.

But there was no more Chinaco. So, being the smart entrepreneur that he is, Bob Denton contracted with long-time tequila maker Don Felipe Camarena to allow him to market his 100 percent agave Tequila Tapatio in the United States under the "El Tesoro de Don Felipe" label. Denton personally took this estate-grown, -distilled, and -bottled superpremium tequila throughout the United States and introduced it to bars, restaurants, and distributors. Perhaps unknowingly, Denton had established the benchmark for superpremium tequila imported into the United States.

While Denton was extolling the virtues of "the treasure" (El Tesoro) of fine estate-grown 100-percent agave tequila, Martin Crowley was making a deal with the makers of Siete

Leguas tequila to produce a 100-percent agave silver and añejo tequila that he could import and market in the United States under the name of "Patrón." Now, once the deal was consummated, Crowley took a giant step forward: he created a never-before-seen package for his tequila. He presented the tequila in a handblown glass decanter bottle with a ball-shaped stopper that by design would catch the eye of consumers in the United States. Not only did his packaging work, but he had (like Denton, perhaps unknowingly) established the benchmark for the new age of packaging tequila—in unusual handblown, interesting-looking glass bottles.

This progression leads us to reemphasize something you really need to be careful about when buying tequila: if it is expensive, first make sure the tequila is 100-percent agave. Second, make sure you're not paying for the bottle. Some of the great tequilas being sold in America today are packaged in great-looking handblown glass bottles, and just because the bottle may be unusual, don't shy away from it. Refer to the tequila descriptions later in this book or ask your liquor dealer about it—most dealers are becoming more and more familiar with superpremium tequilas and can give intelligent guidance to their customers.

By the mid-1990s, Crowley had entered into a distribution agreement with Seagrams, and Denton did the same with the Jim Beam Company. Denton has, in the meantime, managed to restart the production of Chinaco. Unfortunately, the mystique surrounding it has pretty much worn off, but it is a fantastic tequila; ironically, the new Chinaco is marketed in a handsome handblown tear-shaped bottle. These two pioneers have been instrumental in raising the customer's awareness of truly exceptional, superpremium (100-percent agave) tequila, and their role in making tequila the fastest-growing liquor is to be applauded.

Other Essentials for a Great Margarita

A great margarita—a real margarita—must contain three primary ingredients: real tequila, real triple sec, and real freshly squeezed lemon or lime juice. It must also be correctly hand-shaken with ice, not put into a blender. Tequila drinks mixed in a blender, using extra sugar, concentrated lime juice, frozen lemonade, limeade, or a commercial margarita mix, are not real margaritas no matter how good the tequila is. Nothing bothers me more than to see a bar serving margaritas out of a slush-type machine right into the glass (most likely made using a lot of ice, sugar, water, and cheap rotgut tequila). These are not real margaritas!

The variations among the margaritas in this book are created by using different tequilas, different orange liqueurs, and different types of citrus juices to make a real margarita.

The Liqueur

Margaritas are made using one of three different orange liqueurs: triple sec, Cointreau, or Grand Marnier. The combinations of different liqueurs with the many different kinds of tequilas yield a wide variety of subtle variations on the basic margarita.

Triple sec is a clear liqueur made from the skins of Curaçao and other exotic oranges that have been fermented, sun-dried, reconstituted in distilled water, and then triple-distilled. Each of the distillations condenses the natural sugars and removes some of the bitterness of the orange peel. Most commercial triple sec is artificially flavored; be sure to check the label to find one made with all-natural ingredients. Triple secs are usually available in 60 proof or 42 proof. At Maria's we prefer the lower-alcohol-content version with the delicate flavor of tequila. We use Bols brand 42-proof triple sec for several of our margaritas. Bols is a premium-quality triple sec, as are Marie Brizard and DeKuyper.

Cointreau is a superpremium, 80-proof orange liqueur imported from France. It was created in 1849 by Adolphe Cointreau and his brother Edouard, who were candy makers experimenting with fruit and spirits. (It was probably the orange liqueur used to make the original margarita.) Cointreau is a blend of bitter and sweet oranges, grown and selected for their quality in Haiti, Brazil, and Spain. The only part of the orange that is used is the peel, which is laid out to dry in the sun for several days, then sent back to the distillery in Angers, France. There the oil from the peels is blended with grain-neutral spirits and pure cane sugar and distilled three times. Cointreau's distinctive orange flavor is usually the best complement to premium or superpremium tequila. I wouldn't think of using anything other than Cointreau or Grand Marnier with superpremium tequila.

Grand Marnier, another French import, is made by blending superpremium orange liqueur with premium cognac, which is then aged for a minimum of 18 months. At Maria's, we use Grand Marnier to make our Grand Gold Margarita (see page 36), one of the most popular of all our margaritas. Grand Marnier is 80 proof.

If you want a margarita with a lot of character and a completely different "twist," make it with Grand Marnier. The subtle flavor of oranges blends with the hint of cognac and the flavor of the tequila to make quite a statement! However, because the flavor of the Grand Marnier can easily become the dominant flavor of the drink, margaritas made with Cointreau are probably as authentic as you'll want to get. But you can decide for yourself what you like—there are an awful lot of folks that love margaritas made with Grand Marnier.

The Citrus Juice

Based on research we have done on the origins of the margarita (see Chapter 3), I am confident that the original margarita was indeed made with freshly squeezed lime juice. Having said that, I must admit that we use freshly squeezed lemon juice at Maria's.

The reason we use lemon juice is that the quality of fresh limes is just too inconsistent. Depending on the season, we sometimes get limes from Mexico, at other times from California, Florida, or South America, and we are always at the mercy of our suppliers. Sometimes those limes can be so tart you can't stand them, while at other times they'll be as sweet as sugar. By contrast, lemons are considerably more uniform in flavor, regardless of geographical origin or time of year. If you do find a sweet, juicy lime, we'll bet that you can tell little difference in flavor between a margarita made with lemon juice and one made with lime juice. (We do not recommend frozen concentrated lime or lemon juice that has sugar added, but Minute Maid produces a pure, frozen unsweetened lemon juice that may be substituted for fresh.)

We never use commercial margarita mix at Maria's, and we strongly recommend that you avoid it too. We use a commercial sweet-and-sour mix in a margarita only when a customer insists that his or her margarita be frozen and mixed in the blender instead of shaken. The problem with using a blender to make margaritas is that the ice turns to water and overdilutes the cocktail, making it almost flavorless. As convinced as we are at Maria's about what makes a real margarita, we also believe that the customer is always right—even when he or she isn't. So if you want a frozen margarita at Maria's, we will make it for you.

The Salt

Salt is an important element of the margarita. It is never put in the drink itself—it is only used on the rim of the margarita glass. You simply pass a wedge of lemon or lime over the rim of an empty glass, then dip the glass in a saucer of salt.

We use kosher salt because it is additive-free and because the coarser texture has the best consistency. Simple table salt is acceptable, although you will need more of it and it will dissolve quickly. (If using table salt, use less lemon or lime juice on the rim of the glass so that less salt will stick to it.) Inexpensive boxes of kosher salt are available at most grocery stores and will last a very long time.

The Ice

One of the most important ingredients in a real margarita is the ice. The shape and size of the ice cube is important because, as you shake the margarita, the corners of the ice cubes will break off and dilute the other ingredients to just the proper point. "Round ice cubes" are not only an oxymoron, they just don't work in a margarita (they will work, however, if you crack each one). Be careful, since the more you crack and crush your ice, the more you'll dilute your margarita.

You need to use small cubes, ideally about 1 inch (a little smaller will do, but not too much larger than that). If you're using ice out of household refrigerator ice trays, crack it into pieces by tapping the cubes sharply with the back of a tablespoon while cradling them in the palm of your cupped hand. The ideal ice is the commercial type you buy in bags at most grocery, liquor, or convenience stores.

The Equipment

Real margaritas are pretty low-tech, and (you'll be glad to hear) the equipment needed to make them requires little capital. The first things you'll need are a stainless steel cocktail shaker top and a 16-ounce cocktail shaker. Shaking the mixture of tequila, orange liqueur, lemon juice, and ice will break off just the right amount from the corners of the ice for proper dilution of the drink.

Please don't use a blender! All it does is purée everything into a watery slush, diluting the flavor of the tequila and the orange liqueur. The result is a pale version of a margarita that bears little resemblance to the real thing and is a waste of good liquor. The one and only exception to this rule is when making fruit margaritas. Although they're not true margaritas, these are wonderful, refreshing summertime drinks, and sometimes you just can't beat the taste of fresh strawberries, peaches, or apricots. A blender or food processor is a must for making these; just follow the recipes we have provided.

We recommend that margaritas be served "on the rocks" (over ice). We don't think you'll mind the small amount of dilution that occurs during the time it takes to consume your margarita. The drink stays colder longer, and the water added from the melting ice will not affect the flavor of the margarita.

If you prefer your margaritas "up," or without ice, you'll need some sort of a drink strainer (you've probably seen one of those stainless steel things behind the bar that looks like a miniature Ping-Pong paddle with a spring around it). Some of the bartenders at Maria's prefer to strain margaritas by inserting the bottom of the empty shaker top into the shaker glass with the cocktail mixture and pouring the liquid out into a glass. If you do this, you won't need a strainer (which makes a cheap alternative).

We do not serve pitchers of margaritas at Maria's for several reasons that have to do with the practical concerns of running a restaurant. For one thing, margaritas are quite potent. Each one contains a double shot of 80-proof spirits in a drink so smooth and flavorful that when properly made just goes down too easily. If we served entire pitchers of margaritas, we would have a bunch of drunk customers, and that is not our goal. Moreover, an entire pitcher of margaritas sitting on a table would become so diluted from the melted ice that the intended flavor of the margaritas would be destroyed. With that in mind, the only feasible way to maintain the integrity of the margarita's flavor in a pitcher would be to serve it with no ice in the pitcher. If you shook eight margaritas individually and strained out the ice, a 64-ounce pitcher (most of our recipes yield about 8 ounces of liquid each) of one of our premium margaritas would cost over $60 (there's not going to be a lot of takers).

We have had success serving numerous margaritas at one time while maintaining the flavor by following a simple procedure using a large punch bowl. (Every year, we serve our La Ultima Margarita to over 1,000 people at the Santa Fe Buckaroo Ball using a punch bowl and receive rave reviews!) To use a punch bowl, simply add a large chunk of ice (not cubes) after all of the ingredients are in the bowl and mix well. Then stir to create a bit of melting. Using a ladle, pour the margarita mixture into salt-rimmed glasses that have been filled at least three-quarters with ice cubes. The chunk of ice will add the proper amount of water to the concoction; however, if the flavor is a bit tart, add a cup or two of cold water until you get the taste you desire.

If you are entertaining at home and *do* choose to serve by the pitcher, you can hand-shake individual margaritas according to the recipe and strain off the liquid into a chilled pitcher until it's as full as you want it to be. Have an ice bucket handy, along with salt-rimmed glasses. Add the ice to the presalted glasses and pour the margarita from the pitcher. Just remember, half the fun is shaking each cocktail—it's a great way to show off!

We use two different types of glasses for our margaritas. One is the hurricane-style stemmed glass, which is curved like the glass chimney of hurricane lamps; the other is the flat saucer-bowl-type stemmed glass often used for champagne. The hurricane glass is used for margaritas on the rocks, and the saucer-bowl type is used for "up" margaritas.

Any variation of these glasses will do, and the Margarita Police will not hunt you down or press charges if you use a stemless glass. The main requirement is that your glass be big enough to hold the margaritas. As we like to put it, "It ain't what you drink from, it's what you're drinking" (or words to that effect).

The only other piece of equipment you will need is a jigger or other measuring device. All our recipes list the ingredients as ounces or fractions of an ounce (basic bar jiggers come in 3/4-ounce, 1-ounce, 1 1/2-ounce, and 2-ounce sizes). We recommend that you buy a combination stainless steel jigger with one side measuring 3/4 ounce, the other 1 1/4 ounces (you can double the 3/4-ounce side for 1 1/2 ounces, etc.). These jiggers look like hourglasses and should be available at most gourmet cooking or bar supply outlets. If all else fails, just remember than 3/4 ounce equals 1 1/2 tablespoons, 1 ounce equals 2 tablespoons, and 1 1/4 ounces equal 2 1/2 tablespoons.

CHAPTER THREE

The Noble Origins of the Margarita

Who invented the margarita? One might just as easily ask, "Who discovered fire?" The point is, someone, sometime, took the plunge and made a margarita. And, while not as old as fire, its flavor is unique unto itself.

There are several stories (or legends, if you will) as to the origin of the margarita. In order to cover all the bases, we asked a number of food and beverage magazines to print a request for readers' versions of the margarita story. We were surprised both by the number of responses and by the variety of theories out there. Far be it from us to say which story is true; instead, we would like to pass along the most interesting stories so you can come to your own conclusion. The accounts are given in their original versions.

The most commonly related story of the margarita's origin is this one:

Shortly after World War II, corporate America (and Hollywood) discovered Palm Springs, California, as a pleasant and scenic retreat from the hustle and bustle of the big city: play some golf, talk some business, and enjoy some good liquor with the boys. Well, Palm Springs is only a few hours' drive from Mexico and, with this close proximity, a magical "new" liquor, tequila, was discovered by affluent America.

These corporate guys were introduced to tequila the old-fashioned way: a shot of tequila, a lick of salt, and a bit of lime—brings tears to your eyes, doesn't it? The same "good old boys" then started bringing their wives and girlfriends (and no doubt in some cases both) to their little getaway out in the middle of the California desert and, like most men, they wanted to impress the womenfolk with their newly discovered tequila and their macho way of drinking it. Sorry, boys: the shot of tequila, lick of salt, and bite of lime wasn't the ladies' cup of tea.

So along came Jones or Garcia (or whomever—history does not record the creative genius in this version) who concocted a drink that had all of the same elements of the shot of tequila—the liquor, the salt, and the lime—except that Cointreau was added to give the cocktail a little sweetness. This enterprising mixologist created the first margarita by shaking the essential ingredients in a shaker glass over ice, then straining the cocktail into a salt-rimmed glass.

Not only did the women love it, but so did the guys. Although this legend does not name the bartender responsible, it does record that he named his creation after his girlfriend, Margarita. Or, who knows—perhaps the bartender was named Margarita!

Another theory submitted by an advertising agency (published in the fall 1991 edition of the Taylor/Christian Advertising Agency magazine, !deas) identifies a specific woman named Margarita. You probably will not be too surprised to learn that Taylor/Christian Advertising was the agency of record for Cointreau when they published this story:

According to legend, it was during a party at [Margarita Sames's] cliff-side hacienda in Acapulco in 1948 when Margarita began experimenting with "the drink." Cointreau was the key ingredient, and today she scoffs at recipes that call for triple sec. At the party was a group of her closest friends, among them Nicky Hilton of the Hilton Hotel legacy. . . . Margarita was looking for something to cut the dust of a hot December afternoon in Mexico when she stumbled upon "something that kept the party going for two weeks." Margarita's original recipe called for three parts tequila to one part Cointreau and one part lime juice, but being cognizant of America's concern with alcohol, the agency asked her for permission to weaken the mixture. "Okay, as long as you don't use triple sec or blend it up like a Tastee Freeze," she replied tersely. To enjoy Margarita's original Margarita, blend one part tequila, one part fresh lime juice, and one part Cointreau in a shaker of ice. Shake vigorously and pour into a lightly salted glass. Anything else is not the Sames. And, according to Margarita, "not worth its salt."

We heard directly from the folks at Cointreau when they learned about our quest for the origin of the margarita, and they sent us the following letter. (Note the date of the letter—clever, huh? Especially since we sent out our call for margarita legends almost 50 years later! Whether the contents of the letter are true or not, you have to admire Cointreau's enterprising publicity department!)

An article from the July 1991 *Texas Monthly* (submitted by Patrick O'Rourke of Rémy Amerique in Sacramento, California—the U.S. distributor of Cointreau) discusses Mrs. Sames's claim. It also mentions that the owner of the Tail o' the Cock, a Los Angeles restaurant and bar, was a houseguest of Mrs. Sames, hence the theory that the margarita originated there. (The Tail o' the Cock has also been mentioned in other margarita-origin stories.)

This Associated Press obituary, submitted by Evelyn Greenwald of the Los Angeles Public Library's State of California Answer Network, appeared in newspapers all over the country in October 1992:

Dateline: San Diego (AP)—Carlos Herrera, known locally as the man who topped a tequila concoction with salt and called it a Margarita, has died. He was 90. Herrera died Monday at Grossmont Hospital. His daughter, Gloria Amezcua, said he died of natural causes. Herrera's relatives say he invented the drink at Rancho La Gloria, a restaurant

July 13, 1948

Dear Mr. Lacero,

Greetings from Acapulco! Sorry you can't be with us now to enjoy the sunny weather.

Here's a little memento to let you know I'm thinking of you and to tell you about this wonderful new concoction I created. I hope you'll try it yourself. It's delightful! When you taste it, I'll bet you'll feel like you're here.

Last Christmas, I wanted to give my guests something new and very special, so I mixed equal parts of Cointreau (my favorite liqueur), my best tequila and lime juice and served it in champagne glasses with just a dusting of salt on the rims. Everyone raved about "the drink," and how the smooth orange flavor of Cointreau blended with tequila and tart lime juice made a very refreshing cocktail. They all said they'd never tasted anything like it. It just made our holiday celebration!

The best part is that just last week, my husband Bill said we can't call it "the drink" forever, so he presented me with two lovely glasses etched with "Margarita." "Now 'the drink' has a name," he said. Wasn't that sweet?

Try my original, The Original Margarita made with Cointreau. I'm sure you'll find it as special as we all do.

Fondly,
Margarita

P.S. Keep the frame on your desk to remind you of the special times you'll always have with The Original Margarita.

22

he opened in 1935 at his home south of Tijuana. He told friends that it was sometime in 1938 or '39 that he decided to mix a jigger of white tequila with lemon juice, shaved ice, triple sec and—the crowning touch—salt. Local legend has it that one of his customers was a show-girl and sometime actress who called herself Marjorie King. She was allergic to all hard liquor except tequila, and she didn't like to drink that straight. That reputedly sent Herrera to experimenting, and he named the result "Margarita" after the actress, the legend goes.

We thank Thomas Kandziora, the bar manager of the American Legion Post #288 in Cedarburg, Wisconsin, who sent us an abridged version of this article from the *Chicago Tribune*, and Mary Louise Rogers of San Diego who sent a similar article that ran in the *San Diego Tribune*. Mary Louise adds:

I believe this story must have some merit as I remember after arriving in San Diego late in 1958, friends and I made the trek to Rosarito Beach for lobster. There was a favorite bar we stopped at on the old road on our way down, and that was where I first drank a margarita.

Although Herrera was given local credit for the frosty drink, several others have claimed to have invented the margarita, according to *The Dictionary of American Food and Drink* by John F. Mariani, published in 1983. The book doesn't name Herrera, but it says one story traces the birth of the margarita to an unidentified creator near the Caliente Racetrack in the 1930s, the place and time Herrera claimed he first mixed a margarita. (Hmmm . . . we wonder if Mr. Herrera ever worked at a bar at the Caliente Racetrack or in Palm Springs.)

Food writer Colman Andrews sent us this contribution regarding the origin of the margarita:

I think I know what inspired it: the classic '30s cocktail called the Sidecar. The Sidecar was supposedly invented in 1931 at the legendary Harry's New York Bar on the Rue Daunou in Paris. The story is that it was created, and named, for a young American millionaire—there always seems to be a young American millionaire involved in tales of this sort—who liked to tour the drinking places of the French capital in the sidecar of a friend's motorcycle.

As you may well know, the Sidecar is classically made with two ounces of cognac, 1/2 ounce of fresh-squeezed lemon juice, and 1/4 ounce of Cointreau. These ingredients are shaken together with cracked ice and strained into a cocktail glass whose rim has been dipped in sugar. By simply replacing the cognac with tequila and the sugar with salt, you'd have a pretty reasonable Margarita—and I'd bet that some old-

school bartender who knew the Sidecar, and who perhaps had traveled to Mexico where tequila might otherwise be consumed with salt and lime on the side, put various elements together and came up with this classic drink.

I have several cocktail manuals from the 1950s, incidentally, in which neither the Margarita nor tequila itself is mentioned, suggesting that, whenever it might have been invented, it certainly hadn't yet become a standard drink at that time in the United States. Though I'm sure it was around before this, the earliest reference I can find to it in my own library is from the Time-Life volume Wines and Spirits, published in 1968. You might be amused to hear that, in the course of describing the drink, author Alec Waugh states, "Tequila is not a drink that is ever very likely to be popular among Northerners, whose palates have not been hardened by the unrestrained use of chili."

Nicholas Colletti of Pittsburgh, a keen collector of food facts, wrote to us with his theory about the origin of the margarita:

The Margarita was invented by Red Hinton, a bartender in an early Virginia City bar. He named the drink after Margarita Mendes, his Mexican girlfriend. One day, she hit a man over the head with a bottle of whiskey, and his friend, Robert Arthur, got excited and shot off his revolver to scare her away. He accidentally hit her in the top of the head and killed her. However, he was freed, as it was decided that if he had wanted to kill her, he would have aimed at the area that was easiest to hit—her widest area—which in her case happened to be her chest.

The recipe for the original Margarita was as follows: Wet the rim of a glass with the juice of a lemon. Place the rim in a bowl containing salt so the salt sticks to the rim. Put 1 ounce of tequila in a shaker or bowl. Add ½ ounce lemon juice and ½ ounce orange juice. Mix well and pour into the glass. There was no triple sec or ice used to make this drink; there wasn't any in Virginia City when this drink was invented.

Margee Drews from Corona Del Mar, California, wrote to tell us:

I have heard many times that Larry J. Cane, former owner and president of El Torito restaurants, "invented" the blended Margarita as we know it. I've heard that he and a bartender, Barry, blended up a batch in a "slush" type machine. That was over thirty years ago in Los Angeles. [Sorry, Margee—that's not a real margarita; it's a slushee!]

The following information, submitted by Raymond Ritter of Westlake, Ohio, is from The Tequila Book by Marion Gorman and Felipe P. de Alba (Contemporary Books, 1978). One of the theories given regarding the origin of the margarita claims that

Danny Negrete, the manager of the Crespo Hotel in Pueblo, Mexico, created the drink in 1936 for his girlfriend, Margarita:

She habitually took a dab of salt with whatever she had to drink. Danny decided that he would create a drink for her so she could enjoy it without having to reach into the common table salt-bowl; he would put the salt on the rim of her glass. He chose tequila—probably that was Margarita's favorite drink. Then he decided to add Cointreau and lemon [sic] juice and shake it up with ice.

Another theory from the same source names Doña Bertha, owner of a bar in Taxco, Mexico, as the creator of the margarita.

Former Santa Fe restaurateur Walt McDowell wrote to us from Fort Myers, Florida, with a colorful and historical theory:

The sixteenth-century explorer Ponce de Leon traveled to the New World in search of the Fountain of Youth, said to be guarded by a race of ageless giants, the Calusa. While the Fountain of Youth was a myth, the Calusa were indeed a tribe that existed in Florida, and who were not only tall (over six feet) but lived to an estimated eighty to ninety years of age. It is documented that the Calusa, who were trading part-ners with the Mayan civilization of Mexico, were versed in the cultiva-tion of many tropical fruits, including sweet limes.

In 1513, Ponce de Leon made contact with the Calusa but later died in a war he fought against them. Two hundred years later, Ponce de Leon's direct descendant, Margerete, was the wife of a well-known pirate, Don José Gaspar, whose trading booty in the Gulf of Mexico included "cactus whisky," distilled from the agave plant and now known as tequila. Gaspar's favorite drink was sweet lime juice and "cactus whiskey," with a touch of sea salt left on the rim of the mug after it had been washed in sea water. This potion was named by his crew after his wife, Margerete.

Elaine Corn, aptly named food critic, writer, and author, wrote to let us know about Francisco "Pancho" Morales, a bartender from Juarez who claimed to have invented the margarita in 1942:

He [Morales] plied his trade at Tommy's Place, a spot popular with Fort Bliss GIs. This is where the Margarita supposedly first was poured, despite claims to its origin as frequent as Elvis sightings. The first thing to dispel is this: It wasn't named for a woman or child. A 1974 article in Texas Monthly magazine written by El Pasoan Brad Cooper ought to have been the last word on the subject, so thorough is the depiction. Pancho Morales is presented as the clear creator, with paper documentation, convenient timing, and oral testimony. Still,

Cooper carefully constructs his article liberally using the term "supposedly" in almost every reference to anything having to do with the Margarita. . . .

"A lady came in and ordered a Magnolia," Morales told Cooper. The only thing Morales knew about a Magnolia—a true drink known in Juarez bars—was that it had Cointreau, a little lime and some kind of liquor. So, he did what any good bartender would do: He winged it. The woman recognized the fake, but said it was good anyway, probably because Morales had loaded it with enough tequila to make anyone smile. Morales' train of thought had gone to flowers, from magnolia to daisy, which translates in Spanish to Margarita.

The following story was submitted by Ronnie Vaughan, a sales executive for the Albuquerque distributor of José Cuervo tequila. It's from the Cuervo "fact book" provided to salespeople for the National Distributing Company:

Margaritas originated "in heaven," say its most devoted admirers. Other versions of the story vary. One of the best claims has been staked by the Tail o' the Cock restaurant on La Cienega in Los Angeles. The year: 1954. The culprit: the head bartender. The result: if this was indeed a first, a place in beverage history.

A similar story was provided by Lee Spencer:

After the war, Young's Market Company owner Vernon Underwood owned a tequila brand called José Cuervo. They were and still are a major liquor distributor in Los Angeles. At that time, vodka was starting to move due to a popular drink made famous at the Cock and Bull restaurant on Sunset Boulevard, Los Angeles, called Moscow Mule. Underwood took his tequila to his friend McHenry, who owned the Tail o' the Cock restaurant. They gave it to his bartender, who put together a concoction using lime juice and Curaçao. The results were great, so a name was needed. They asked the bartender, who said: "My wife's name is Margaret. Why not call it a Margarita, Spanish for Margaret?" The rest is history.

An article submitted by Dennis Hamann, printed in a beverage trade magazine in 1969, mentions the same Vernon Underwood, then-president of the Young Market Company. In this version, Underwood was curious to know why the Tail o' the Cock restaurant was suddenly ordering five cases of tequila at a time, during a period when tequila sales were relatively dormant. He found that the bartender had invented the Margarita, using Underwood's Cuervo tequila, and that this cocktail was rapidly winning acclaim by word of mouth. As a result, Underwood's company launched the first tequila advertising campaign with the theme, "Margarita is more than just a girl's name," with emphasis on the fact that the jet set had taken to drinking margaritas in posh surroundings wearing white ties and tails.

Another article submitted by Glen "The Bartender" Steward, from Las Vegas, Nevada, repeats the claim that Carlos Herrera (see page 21) invented the margarita and named it after a showgirl, Marjorie King (although in this version, Herrera's first name is Danny). The article then quotes Herrera as saying, "The Mexican bartender at the Tail o' the Cock in Los Angeles was a friend, and I told him how to make it [the Margarita]. . . . One day I walked in there and he said, 'Danny, look around. Everybody's drinking Margaritas.'"

Could this be the missing link between all these stories?

There are probably two or three dozen more stories about how the margarita was invented. You might even know one of them. One problem in pinning down the origins of the margarita is that, whatever you name the drink, tequila mixes so naturally and appealingly with citrus juices that it was bound to happen sooner or later, and perhaps sooner even than we think. The bottom line is, the margarita was invented and, with some variations, it is the same (or we think it is the same) as it has been since the late 1930s (or late '40s, depending on whom you believe). It is significant that one common denominator in all the margarita stories is the fact that no sugars are ever used, only unsweetened citrus juices. Regardless of what type of margarita you are making, the sweetness should consist solely of the natural sweetness of the blue agave nectar that has been fermented and double-distilled into tequila and the orange liqueur that is mixed with it.

CHAPTER FOUR

Recipes for
Real Margaritas

The great margarita recipes in this chapter are organized by tequila manufacturer and then by type. For example, we begin with margaritas made with Cuervo tequila, from the mass-market Cuervo Silver up to the superpremium Cuervo Tradicional Reserva de la Familia añejo. Then we present margaritas made with Sauza tequila, from Sauza Silver to Sauza Hornitos Reposado, and so on. The margarita recipes at the beginning of this chapter use premium tequilas, while those toward the end use super-premium tequilas.

The recipes in this chapter feature virtually all of the real tequilas currently available on the American market. In some cases we use the same tequila for two margarita recipes, altering the taste of the drink by changing the orange liqueur. You will note that some brands of tequila are used in many more recipes than are others. This is due to the popularity of the margaritas at Maria's. While all of our margaritas are real, not all are in an equal state of demand.

Each section begins with a brief discussion of the tequila manufacturer and the various tequilas under that name. Information on the specific tequila used in each margarita appears in the headnote for each recipe. In addition, the Resources list (page 150) provides a source in case a certain tequila is unavailable in your local liquor store.

Cuervo

The name José Cuervo is virtually synonymous with tequila. Truly, Cuervo is the world's premier tequila distiller. They produce a wide array of premium and super-premium tequilas and export more than 1 million cases of tequilas to the United States annually. Their Cuervo Silver is the number-one best-selling tequila in the United States. (If your liquor or grocery store doesn't stock Cuervo, it's time to change stores!)

MARIA'S SPECIAL MARGARITA
Makes 1 margarita

Maria's Special Margarita is made with Cuervo Silver and is the number-one best-selling hand-shaken margarita in Santa Fe.

1 lemon or lime wedge
Saucer of kosher salt (about ¼-inch deep)
1¼ ounces José Cuervo Silver tequila
1 ounce Bols triple sec
1½ ounces freshly squeezed lemon or lime juice
Ice

Run the lemon or lime wedge around the rim of a hurricane-style margarita glass. Dip the rim of the glass into the saucer of salt, rotating the rim in the salt until the desired amount has collected on the glass.

Measure the tequila, triple sec, and lemon or lime juice into a 16-ounce cocktail shaker glass full of ice. Place a stainless steel cocktail shaker over the glass, tapping the top to create a seal. Shake vigorously for about 5 seconds and pour into the salt-rimmed glass.

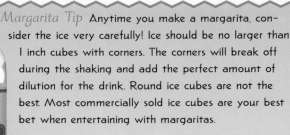

Margarita Tip Anytime you make a margarita, consider the ice very carefully! Ice should be no larger than 1 inch cubes with corners. The corners will break off during the shaking and add the perfect amount of dilution for the drink. Round ice cubes are not the best. Most commercially sold ice cubes are your best bet when entertaining with margaritas.

Tequila Tidbit The United States is the biggest consumer of tequila (even outselling Mexico!), with imports more than double the consumption in Mexico itself. The third largest consumer of tequila is Germany.

THE CUERVO GOLD MARGARITA
Makes 1 margarita

Tequila Cuervo Especial, commonly called José Cuervo Gold, is perhaps the best known of all tequilas sold in the United States—it's the one that Jimmy Buffett refers to in his classic "Margaritaville" recording.

> 1 lemon or lime wedge
> Saucer of kosher salt (about ¼-inch deep)
> 1¼ ounces Tequila Cuervo Especial (Premium Gold)
> 1 ounce Bols triple sec
> 1½ ounces freshly squeezed lemon or lime juice
> Ice

Run the lemon or lime wedge around the rim of a hurricane-style margarita glass. Dip the rim of the glass into the saucer of salt, rotating the rim in the salt until the desired amount has collected on the glass.

Measure the tequila, triple sec, and lemon or lime juice into a 16-ounce cocktail shaker glass full of ice. Place a stainless steel cocktail shaker over the glass, tapping the top to create a seal. Shake vigorously for about 5 seconds and pour into the salt-rimmed glass.

Tequila Tidbit The Cuervo family produced mezcal before they distilled tequila. Their mezcal business dates from the late 1700s; tequila was introduced in the last half of the 19th century.

THE RAFAEL MARGARITA

Makes 1 margarita

The Rafael, or "Ralph," is a longtime favorite of Maria's old-timers and was in fact named after a patron named Ralph, who asked our bartender to make a margarita according to this recipe. This margarita differs from the earlier recipes by combining an inexpensive premium gold tequila (Tequila Cuervo Especial) with Cointreau, an expensive superpremium orange liqueur.

1 lemon or lime wedge
Saucer of kosher salt (about ¼-inch deep)
1¼ ounces Tequila Cuervo Especial Gold tequila
1 ounce Cointreau
1½ ounces freshly squeezed lemon or lime juice
Ice

Run the lemon or lime wedge around the rim of a hurricane-style margarita glass. Dip the rim of the glass into the saucer of salt, rotating the rim in the salt until the desired amount has collected on the glass.

Measure the tequila, Cointreau, and lemon or lime juice into a 16-ounce cocktail shaker glass full of ice. Place a stainless steel cocktail shaker over the glass, tapping the top to create a seal. Shake vigorously for about 5 seconds and pour into the salt-rimmed glass.

Margarita Tip As we progress with the margarita recipes in this book, you will notice that while the ingredients remain proportionately consistent, the combinations of ingredients change subtly. For example, we not only use different tequilas, but different combinations of triple sec, Cointreau, and Grand Marnier.

Tequila Tidbit The town of Tequila is located 40 miles northwest of Guadalajara and has a population of 25,000. The name means "lava hill" in the Nahuatl Indian (Aztec) language, but these native people had vanished by 1656, when a Spanish settlement was permanently established. "Lava hill" refers to the fact that the town sits on the lower slopes of an extinct volcano.

THE 1812 OVERTURE MARGARITA
Makes 1 margarita

This margarita derives its name from Cuervo's 1800 brand of tequila (what's 12 years between friends?) and the fact that this tequila, mixed with Cointreau, truly conjures up an overture of flavor. One of the most popular premium tequilas made by Cuervo, José Cuervo 1800 comes in a decanter-type bottle.

> 1 lemon or lime wedge
> Saucer of kosher salt (about ¼-inch deep)
> 1¼ ounces José Cuervo 1800 tequila
> 1 ounce Cointreau
> 1½ ounces freshly squeezed lemon or lime juice
> Ice

Run the lemon or lime wedge around the rim of a hurricane-style margarita glass. Dip the rim of the glass into the saucer of salt, rotating the rim in the salt until the desired amount has collected on the glass.

Measure the tequila, triple sec, and lemon or lime juice into a 16-ounce cocktail shaker glass full of ice. Place a stainless steel cocktail shaker over the glass, tapping the top to create a seal. Shake vigorously for about 5 seconds and pour into the salt-rimmed glass.

Tequila Tidbit There are many popular songs that extol the virtues of tequila. In the 1950s, the Champs recorded "Tequila." The Eagles are famous for their "Tequila Sunrise," and we've already mentioned Jimmy Buffett's "Margaritaville." There's also Bobby Bare's "Pour Me Another Tequila, Sheila," but perhaps while you sip this particular cocktail, you'd like to hum along with Shelley West's classic, "José Cuervo, You Are a Friend of Mine."

THE GRAND GOLD MARGARITA
Makes 1 margarita

We use the same Cuervo Premium gold tequila for this recipe as for the previous Cuervo Gold Margarita, but Grand Marnier rather than triple sec. This gives the cocktail a sweeter, more intense flavor.

1 lemon or lime wedge
Saucer of kosher salt (about ¼-inch deep)
1¼ ounces Tequila Cuervo Especial (premium gold)
    tequila
1 ounce Grand Marnier
1½ ounces freshly squeezed lemon or lime juice
Ice

Run the lemon or lime wedge around the rim of a hurricane-style margarita glass. Dip the rim of the glass into the saucer of salt, rotating the rim in the salt until the desired amount has collected on the glass.

Measure the tequila, Grand Marnier, and lemon or lime juice into a 16-ounce cocktail shaker glass full of ice. Place a stainless steel cocktail shaker over the glass, tapping the top to create a seal. Shake vigorously for about 5 seconds and pour into the salt-rimmed glass.

Tequila Tidbit To understand the scale of the largest producers in the tequila market, it may come as no surprise to learn that over a third of all tequila is produced by the Cuervo distillery. This is twice as much as Sauza, the next largest producer. In turn, Sauza is twice as large as the third biggest producer.

THE JOSÉ CUERVO TRADICIONAL MARGARITA

Makes 1 margarita

Cuervo, the leading tequila producer in the world, has now brought out a limited production of Tequila José Cuervo Tradicional, a superpremium 100-percent agave reposado tequila (aged in oak barrels for at least 60 days). It is wonderfully smooth, with a delightful nose and flavor.

> 1 lemon or lime wedge
> Saucer of kosher salt (about ¼-inch deep)
> 1¼ ounces José Cuervo Tradicional 100-percent agave
>   reposado tequila
> 1 ounce Cointreau
> 1½ ounces freshly squeezed lemon or lime juice
> Ice

Run the lemon or lime wedge around the rim of a hurricane-style margarita glass. Dip the rim of the glass into the saucer of salt, rotating the rim in the salt until the desired amount has collected on the glass.

Measure the tequila, Cointreau, and lemon or lime juice into a 16-ounce cocktail shaker glass full of ice. Place a stainless steel cocktail shaker over the glass, tapping the top to create a seal. Shake vigorously for about 5 seconds and pour into the salt-rimmed glass.

Margarita Tip At Maria's, we have strong feelings about commercial margarita mixes. Don't waste good money on them when the best ingredients you can use—fresh lemons and limes—costs only pennies per drink.

Tequila Tidbit Each bottle of Cuervo Tradicional is individually numbered. For some time, Cuervo bottled this fine tequila only in 375-ml bottles, but now they are also bottling this tequila in the industry norm: 750-ml bottles.

THE 1800 MASTERPIECE MARGARITA
Makes 1 margarita

José Cuervo introduced this new 100-percent agave añejo tequila in 1998 in the same shaped bottle as their popular 1800 tequila (which is not 100-percent agave). When asked if they were phasing out the Cuervo 1800, they told us, "no, but we are going to have a new line of tequilas called '1800'." If our original margarita made with Cuervo 1800 was an overture (see page 35), then a margarita made with the new 100-percent agave 1800 tequila is indeed a masterpiece—hence the name.

  1 lemon or lime wedge
  Saucer of kosher salt (about ¼-inch deep)
  1¼ ounces Reserva Antigua 1800 100-percent agave
    añejo tequila
  1 ounce Cointreau
  1½ ounces freshly squeezed lemon or lime juice
  Ice

Run the lemon or lime wedge around the rim of a hurricane-style margarita glass. Dip the rim of the glass into the saucer of salt, rotating the rim in the salt until the desired amount has collected on the glass.

Measure the tequila, Cointreau, and lemon or lime juice into a 16-ounce cocktail shaker glass full of ice. Place a stainless steel cocktail shaker over the glass, tapping the top to create a seal. Shake vigorously for about 5 seconds and pour into the salt-rimmed glass.

Tequila Tidbit Don't confuse Cuervo's regular 1800 tequila with the Reserva Antigua 1800 Añejo. Remember, if a tequila is 100-percent agave, then it has to say so somewhere on the bottle. The Reserva Antigua 1800 Añejo says it . . . the Cuervo 1800 does not.

THE 24-KARAT GOLD RESERVA MARGARITA
Makes 1 margarita

Three-hundred-fifty years in the making! We combine 200th Anniversary Hand Crafted José Cuervo Reserva de la Familia 100-percent añejo barrel select tequila with 150th Anniversary Cuvee Speciale Centcinquantenaire Grand Marnier (plus freshly squeezed lemon juice) to make this solid gold concoction. This tequila comes in a handblown bottle inside a colorful wooden box and will rival any cognac for sipping from a brandy snifter.

> 1 lemon or lime wedge
> Saucer of kosher salt (about ¼-inch deep)
> 1¼ ounces José Cuervo Reserva de la Familia
>   100-percent agave añejo tequila
> 1 ounce 150th Anniversary Cuvee Speciale
>   Centcinquantenaire Grand Marnier
> 1½ ounces freshly squeezed lemon or lime juice
> Ice

Run the lemon or lime wedge around the rim of a hurricane-style margarita glass. Dip the rim of the glass into the saucer of salt, rotating the rim in the salt until the desired amount has collected on the glass.

Measure the tequila, Grand Marnier, and lemon or lime juice into a 16-ounce cocktail shaker glass full of ice. Place a stainless steel cocktail shaker over the glass, tapping the top to create a seal. Shake vigorously for about 5 seconds and pour into the salt-rimmed glass.

Tequila Tidbit The blue agave plant is a succulent and belongs to the lily family. Its full botanical name is **Agave Tequilana Weber**, named after the botanist (Weber) who classified the plant.

Margarita Tip The ingredients in this margarita are expensive (we sell this margarita for $29 at Maria's), but for that special occasion, it is worth every penny. With a tequila this good on its own, imagine how good the margarita will be . . . and when you add the 150th Anniversary Grand Marnier (also super sippin' stuff), voilà!

Sauza

The Sauza distillery, located in the town of Tequila, Jalisco, is one of the most modern of tequila plants, using cutting-edge cooking and recovery techniques they've developed over the years. Sauza claims that Sauza Silver tequila is the traditional favorite and largest-selling tequila in Mexico. (Cuervo claims the same about their tequila for the United States.)

THE SAUZA SILVER MARGARITA
Makes 1 margarita

Tequila aficionados will debate whether Sauza Silver or Cuervo Silver is the best popularly priced tequila sold in the United States. Both are excellent products—I suggest you try both and decide for yourself (as if you need an excuse to taste-test!).

> 1 lemon or lime wedge
> Saucer of kosher salt (about ¼-inch deep)
> 1¼ ounces Sauza Silver tequila
> 1 ounce Bols triple sec
> 1½ ounces freshly squeezed lemon or lime juice
> Ice

Run the lemon or lime wedge around the rim of a hurricane-style margarita glass. Dip the rim of the glass into the saucer of salt, rotating the rim in the salt until the desired amount has collected on the glass.

Measure the tequila, triple sec, and lemon or lime juice into a 16-ounce cocktail shaker glass full of ice. Place a stainless steel cocktail shaker over the glass, tapping the top to create a seal. Shake vigorously for about 5 seconds and pour into the salt-rimmed glass.

Margarita Tip Attention all readers with a sweet tooth! The natural sugars in the ingredients listed in these recipes should be more than enough to satisfy even those with the sweetest of sweet-tooths. If you're used to drinking extremely sweet margaritas, however, ours may seem a bit dry to you. But hey, these are real margaritas, so we urge you to try a few of our recipes. We are sure that you'll never stray back to icky-sweet fake margaritas again!

Tequila Tidbit American vendors tend to rank liquor quality in terms of premium and superpremium. Tequilas that comply with the Mexican government's strict regulations, such as José Cuervo or Sauza tequila, are considered premium because they contain at least 51-percent agave sugars. The tequilas made from 100-percent agave sugar, such as Herradura, El Tesoro, and Centinela, are considered superpremium.

THE SAUZA GOLD MARGARITA
Makes 1 margarita

This margarita is made with one of the most popular tequilas used in Mexico: Sauza Tequila Especial, Tipo de Oro ("gold type"). You'll notice that the most reputable distillers, like Sauza, will not try to mislead the public by calling a fresh tequila with caramel coloring "añejo," which derives its golden color from aging in oak barrels.

1 lemon or lime wedge
Saucer of kosher salt (about ¼-inch deep)
1¼ ounces Sauza Gold tequila
1 ounce Bols triple sec
1½ ounces freshly squeezed lemon or lime juice
Ice

Run the lemon or lime wedge around the rim of a hurricane-style margarita glass. Dip the rim of the glass into the saucer of salt, rotating the rim in the salt until the desired amount has collected on the glass.

Measure the tequila, triple sec, and lemon or lime juice into a 16-ounce cocktail shaker glass full of ice. Place a stainless steel cocktail shaker over the glass, tapping the top to create a seal. Shake vigorously for about 5 seconds and pour into the salt-rimmed glass.

Tequila Tidbit Tequila can only be produced in very defined regions of five states in Mexico. Only in the state of Jalisco is tequila production allowed throughout the entire state. All 100-percent agave tequila must be produced and bottled in the region of the origin.

THE THREE G's MARGARITA
Makes 1 margarita

The "Three G's" in the title refers to Sauza's Tres Generaciones (Three Generations) Tequila Añejo, an aged tequila produced to honor the successive tequila makers of the Sauza family since 1873: Don Cenobio, Don Eladio, and Don Javier Sauza. This tequila, like all añejos, must be aged in inspector-sealed oak barrels for more than 1 year. Because of this, the tequila is a pale golden color that is acquired naturally from the barrels during the aging process.

> 1 lemon or lime wedge
> Saucer of kosher salt (about ¼-inch deep)
> 1¼ ounces Sauza Tres Generaciones Tequila Añejo
> 1 ounce Cointreau
> 1½ ounces freshly squeezed lemon or lime juice
> Ice

Run the lemon or lime wedge around the rim of a hurricane-style margarita glass. Dip the rim of the glass into the saucer of salt, rotating the rim in the salt until the desired amount has collected on the glass.

Measure the tequila, Cointreau, and lemon or lime juice into a 16-ounce cocktail shaker glass full of ice. Place a stainless steel cocktail shaker over the glass, tapping the top to create a seal. Shake vigorously for about 5 seconds and pour into the salt-rimmed glass.

Margarita Tip Some bars serve margaritas with a straw. Heck, we do this at Maria's. The straw should be used to stir rather than for sipping the cocktail. Margaritas should be sipped from the rim of the glass, through the salt.

Tequila Tidbit Most aged tequilas are placed in oak barrels (most often old, used Kentucky whiskey barrels) for the aging process. Mexican government inspectors seal these barrels when the tequila is put down and must be present when the seal is broken by the producer to bottle the product.

THE HORNY TOAD MARGARITA
Makes 1 margarita

Horny toad is slang for "horned toad," a creature found in abundance in the high desert terrain around Santa Fe. Maria's sells a lot of these margaritas just because of the name (usually, the wife or girlfriend orders it while smiling at the husband or boyfriend and saying something like, "BOY, was this one named after you!"). It also happens to be one of the best margaritas at Maria's. "Hornitos" in Spanish means "little ovens" and refers to the ovens in which the agave piñas are cooked.

> 1 lemon or lime wedge
> Saucer of kosher salt (about ¼-inch deep)
> 1¼ ounces Sauza Hornitos 100-percent agave reposado tequila
> 1 ounce Cointreau
> 1½ ounces freshly squeezed lemon or lime juice
> Ice

Run the lemon or lime wedge around the rim of a hurricane-style margarita glass. Dip the rim of the glass into the saucer of salt, rotating the rim in the salt until the desired amount has collected on the glass.

Measure the tequila, Cointreau, and lemon or lime juice into a 16-ounce cocktail shaker glass full of ice. Place a stainless steel cocktail shaker over the glass, tapping the top to create a seal. Shake vigorously for about 5 seconds and pour into the salt-rimmed glass.

Tequila Tidbit Hornitos is one of Sauza's oldest and most venerable tequilas. It is a 100-percent blue agave tequila reposado (aged no less than 3 months and up to 1 year in oak barrels). Because of the slight aging, Hornitos reposado is slightly darker in color than the silver tequila, and as with most 100-percent agave tequila that has been aged, no artificial coloring has been added.

THE SAUZA CONMEMORATIVO MARGARITA

Makes 1 margarita

Sauza tequila is the major rival to Cuervo, in terms of volume and market share, and the Conmemorativo brand was introduced in an attempt to compete with the premium tequilas that Cuervo has been placing in the American market. It is a delightfully smooth añejo tequila, and even though it is bulk-shipped to Greenwich, Connecticut, for bottling, it is difficult to tell that this tequila is not 100-percent blue agave.

> 1 lemon or lime wedge
> Saucer of kosher salt (about ¼-inch deep)
> 1¼ ounces Sauza Conmemorativo añejo tequila
> 1 ounce Cointreau
> 1½ ounces freshly squeezed lemon or lime juice
> Ice

Run the lemon or lime wedge around the rim of a hurricane-style margarita glass. Dip the rim of the glass into the saucer of salt, rotating the rim in the salt until the desired amount has collected on the glass.

Measure the tequila, Cointreau, and lemon or lime juice into a 16-ounce cocktail shaker glass full of ice. Place a stainless steel cocktail shaker over the glass, tapping the top to create a seal. Shake vigorously for about 5 seconds and pour into the salt-rimmed glass.

Margarita Tip Tequila is 80 proof (the "proof" is double the percentage of the alcohol in the liquor, so 80 proof means that 40 percent of the volume is alcohol). Triple sec is usually 60 proof, but it can be 42 proof. Cointreau and Grand Marnier are 80 proof. All this means that when you combine tequila with one of these liqueurs, you are serving a double—the same thing as serving a double shot of 80-proof whiskey, for example. So consume margaritas (like all other alcohol) responsibly and in moderation.

Tequila Tidbit Only 100-percent agave tequila is required to state the agave percentage on the label. Any other tequila that is at least 51-percent agave does not have to. Some tequilas are obviously more than 51-percent agave, but you'll never know just by reading the label.

LO MEJOR DE SAUZA
Makes 1 margarita

Sauza is not to be outdone by the small boutique distillers. Even though they have been exporting their popularly priced 100-percent agave reposado, Hornitos, for some time, they are entering the super-premium market with a big hit, Galardon. Galardon is a quality 100-percent agave reposado tequila that is being marketed in an attractive tin-wrapped bottle boasting that it is "limited production." The other interesting thing about the label is that Sauza is calling Galardon "gran reposado." There is no official designation for "gran reposado." In my opinion, this is the best of all the Sauza line.

    1 lemon or lime wedge
    Saucer of kosher salt (about ¼-inch deep)
    1¼ ounces Tequila Sauza Galardon 100-percent agave
        gran reposado tequila
    1 ounce Cointreau
    1½ ounces freshly squeezed lemon or lime juice
    Ice

Run the lemon or lime wedge around the rim of a hurricane-style margarita glass. Dip the rim of the glass into the saucer of salt, rotating the rim in the salt until the desired amount has collected on the glass.

Measure the tequila, Cointreau, and lemon or lime juice into a 16-ounce cocktail shaker glass full of ice. Place a stainless steel cocktail shaker over the glass, tapping the top to create a seal. Shake vigorously for about 5 seconds and pour into the salt-rimmed glass.

Tequila Tidbit Ancient murals dating back to approximately 200 A.D. can be found at the site of the Great Pyramid of Cholula near Mexico City. These murals depict the Aztec Indians celebrating by drinking what is commonly believed to be the ancestor of modern tequila. It was probably what is now called **pulque**, which is fermented undistilled agave juice.

Margarita Tip When ordering a margarita at a bar or a restaurant, make sure they are using quality ingredients. You may want to specify 100-percent agave tequila (ask the waiter or bartender to show you the bottle) and Cointreau. Most importantly, if they are using a sweet-and-sour or sweetened mix, ask them to instead squeeze lemons or limes for you and shake the drink and serve it "on the rocks."

Chinaco

When Chinaco 100-percent agave tequila first arrived in the United States in 1983, it created a new category within the tequila industry. Immediately Chinaco built a reputation for itself among the true connoisseurs of tequila. After the distillery was closed in the late 1980s and the tequila went out of production, Chinaco became the most sought-after tequila ever produced. Then, in the mid-1990s, after super effort, it's original importer, Bob Denton, convinced the four sons of the founder, Guillermo Gonzalez, to rekindle La Gonzaleña distillery to once again produce this legendary tequila in very limited quantities. Now in full production, Chinaco is readily available, and because it's distributed by Jim Beam, it should be available most anywhere. The new handblown glass teardrop bottles are very attractive. Chinaco produces only 100-percent agave tequilas and offers a blanco, a reposado, and a well-aged añejo. The Chinaco añejo was first reintroduced to the United States at the 1996 Santa Fe Restaurant Association's Culinary Arts Ball in Santa Fe.

LA MARGARITA DEL CHINACO BLANCO

Makes 1 margarita

The legendary Chinaco 100-percent agave tequilas have always been regarded as a sipping tequila, and some folks would never have considered using it to make margaritas. On the other hand, we at Maria's couldn't wait. And were we rewarded! The blanco-style tequila used in this recipe is bottled fresh out of the still, with no aging on oak, and the natural flavors of the agave come through with flying colors. Mix this one up and you'll agree that adding the Cointreau and freshly squeezed lemon juice makes this one of the most complex yet flavorful margaritas you've ever tasted.

> 1 lemon or lime wedge
> Saucer of kosher salt (about ¼-inch deep)
> 1¼ ounces Chinaco 100-percent agave blanco tequila
> 1 ounce Cointreau
> 1½ ounces freshly squeezed lemon or lime juice
> Ice

Run the lemon or lime wedge around the rim of a hurricane-style margarita glass. Dip the rim of the glass into the saucer of salt, rotating the rim in the salt until the desired amount has collected on the glass.

Measure the tequila, Cointreau, and lemon or lime juice into a 16-ounce cocktail shaker glass full of ice. Place a stainless steel cocktail shaker over the glass, tapping the top to create a seal. Shake vigorously for about 5 seconds and pour into the salt-rimmed glass.

Tequila Tidbit The blue agave cactus grows best in the elevated altitude and dry volcanic soil of West Central Mexico. Another major crop in the region is sugar cane, which is also used by some brands in the tequila-making process.

LA MARGARITA DEL CHINACO PURO
Makes 1 margarita

Take one of the best 100-percent agave tequilas ever made out of the still and lay it down on oak for up to a year, bottle it, and it's just got to be Chinaco 100-percent agave reposado tequila. Now that we've got a great tequila, let's mix it with Cointreau and freshly squeezed lemon juice and see what we get. In this case, it's one of the most unusual margaritas on our list: lots of agave nose coming through the ice and spicy on the palate—more so than with any of our other tequilas.

>   1 lemon or lime wedge
>   Saucer of kosher salt (about ¼-inch deep)
>   1¼ ounces Chinaco 100-percent agave reposado tequila
>   1 ounce Cointreau
>   1½ ounces freshly squeezed lemon or lime juice
>   Ice

Run the lemon or lime wedge around the rim of a hurricane-style margarita glass. Dip the rim of the glass into the saucer of salt, rotating the rim in the salt until the desired amount has collected on the glass.

Measure the tequila, Cointreau, and lemon or lime juice into a 16-ounce cocktail shaker glass full of ice. Place a stainless steel cocktail shaker over the glass, tapping the top to create a seal. Shake vigorously for about 5 seconds and pour into the salt-rimmed glass.

Margarita Tip Most Americans expect froth on a margarita. If it's an authentic margarita, made from the ingredients listed in these recipes, however, there will be little or no froth (although there may be a few bubbles on top when it's poured into a glass). The froth on most cocktails is usually engineered by bartenders who use (surprise!) a frothing ingredient such as a powder made from egg whites or a mix that includes ingredients for this purpose. So remember, if you are drinking a frothy margarita, it's not a real margarita—and you are consuming additives that you don't need.

Tequila Tidbit In this recipe, the Chinaco reposado meets the challenge of the Cointreau and lemon juice to dominate the flavor like no other. Give it a try. If there's such a thing as a macho margarita, this is it—but then, we are using Chinaco.

EL CHINACO CLASSICO MARGARITA
Makes 1 margarita

Maria's Real Margarita List (our menu of margaritas) calls this one "a true delight!" How could it be anything else, given the ingredients? Here we use Chinaco añejo tequila, which has been carefully aged for up to 4 years in government-sealed and -certified oak barrels, enriching the tequila with the characteristics and elegance of a fine cognac. Then, we compliment the Chinaco añejo with not just any Grand Marnier, but the 100th Anniversary Centenaire Grand Marnier. This margarita will cost you nearly $20 at Maria's—try it and see if you think it's worth it.

> 1 lemon or lime wedge
> Saucer of kosher salt (about ¼-inch deep)
> 1¼ ounces Chinaco 100-percent agave añejo tequila
> 1 ounce 100th Anniversary Centenaire Grand Marnier
> 1½ ounces freshly squeezed lemon or lime juice
> Ice

Run the lemon or lime wedge around the rim of a hurricane-style margarita glass. Dip the rim of the glass into the saucer of salt, rotating the rim in the salt until the desired amount has collected on the glass.

Measure the tequila, Grand Marnier, and lemon or lime juice into a 16-ounce cocktail shaker glass full of ice. Place a stainless steel cocktail shaker over the glass, tapping the top to create a seal. Shake vigorously for about 5 seconds and pour into the salt-rimmed glass.

Tequila Tidbit Ninety percent of all tequila exported to the United States from Mexico is transported not in the bottle, but by bulk tanker. Most of this tequila is distilled by Cuervo and Sauza.

EL GRAN CHINACO MARGARITA
Makes 1 margarita

*Mix Chinaco 100-percent agave reposado tequila and Grand Marnier
with freshly squeezed lemon or lime juice, stick to our recipe, and you'll
come up with one of the most elegant margaritas you've ever tasted.
This one is not for wimps. The cognaclike nature of Chinaco reposado
that has been aged for up to 1 year, combined with the touch of premium cognac used to fortify the orange liqueur in the Grand Marnier,
gives this margarita a "stronger" flavor than most of the other recipes
in the book. It may not be as smooth and fruity-sweet as others, but it
sure is a Grand margarita!*

> 1 lemon or lime wedge
> Saucer of kosher salt (about ¼-inch deep)
> 1¼ ounces of Chinaco 100-percent agave reposado
>   tequila
> 1 ounce Grand Marnier
> 1½ ounces freshly squeezed lemon or lime juice
> Ice

Run the lemon or lime wedge around the rim of a hurricane-
style margarita glass. Dip the rim of the glass into the saucer
of salt, rotating the rim in the salt until the desired amount
has collected on the glass.

    Measure the tequila, Grand Marnier, and lemon or lime
juice into a 16-ounce cocktail shaker glass full of ice. Place a
stainless steel cocktail shaker over the glass, tapping the top
to create a seal. Shake vigorously for about 5 seconds and
pour into the salt-rimmed glass.

Margarita Tip If you are having a party, or plan on serving
margaritas to a large group of people, you may want to presalt
a number of glasses. The way we do it at Marias (where we
serve as many as 3,000 margaritas in a week) is to place a
clean, thin sponge on a saucer and moisten it with
fresh lemon or lime juice. Turn a glass upside down
and press the rim down on the sponge to moisten it.
Then dip the rim into a saucer of kosher salt and
rotate the rim until the desired amount of salt has
collected on the glass.

Tequila Tidbit Tequila aficionados will tell
you that the superpremium 100 percent
agave tequilas will not give you a hangover.
This is not true for the premium tequilas that
also contain cane sugar.

Herradura

Herradura is estate-bottled by the Romo family in the foothills of the Sierra Madre mountains of Jalisco. The estate dates back to 1870, and Herradura tequila has been produced by five successive generations. Besides being the first superpremium tequila imported into the United States, Herradura Gold has long served as a quality standard for the Mexican tequila industry.

THE SILVER HERRADURA MARGARITA

Makes 1 margarita

Herradura was one of the first 100-percent agave tequilas imported into the United States and is still the number one selling superpremium brand in the country.

> 1 lemon or lime wedge
> Saucer of kosher salt (about ¼-inch deep)
> 1¼ ounces Herradura Silver Natural tequila
> 1 ounce Bols triple sec
> 1½ ounces freshly squeezed lemon or lime juice
> Ice

Run the lemon or lime wedge around the rim of a hurricane-style margarita glass. Dip the rim of the glass into the saucer of salt, rotating the rim in the salt until the desired amount has collected on the glass.

Measure the tequila, triple sec, and lemon or lime juice into a 16-ounce cocktail shaker glass full of ice. Place a stainless steel cocktail shaker over the glass, tapping the top to create a seal. Shake vigorously for about 5 seconds and pour into the salt-rimmed glass.

Tequila Tidbit We like the rich, natural flavor of Bols triple sec, but there are other brands on the market. If you are considering buying another brand, be sure to read the label. We recommend only investing in a triple sec that uses the natural flavors of exotic oranges and orange peel. Definitely avoid those that contain artificial flavors.

THE HERRADURA FUERTE MARGARITA
Makes 1 margarita

"Fuerte" means strong. Alcoholic spirits are measured for their strength by the "proof," which is double their percentage of alcohol. Thus, a 100-proof liquor is 50 percent alcohol (table wine is usually 12 to 14 percent alcohol). The higher the proof, the stronger the drink. Almost all tequilas, like most other alcoholic spirits, are 80 proof. Well, with that lesson under our belts, we come to the reason for naming this margarita "The Herradura Fuerte." Herradura has begun bottling a tequila called "Herradura Blanco," which is 92 proof, and it is indeed 15 percent stronger than our other tequilas. This, then, is the strong Herradura margarita—La Margarita Herradura Fuerte.

> 1 lemon or lime wedge
> Saucer of kosher salt (about ¼-inch deep)
> 1¼ ounces Herradura 100-percent agave blanco tequila
> 1 ounce Cointreau
> 1½ ounces freshly squeezed lemon or lime juice
> Ice

Run the lemon or lime wedge around the rim of a hurricane-style margarita glass. Dip the rim of the glass into the saucer of salt, rotating the rim in the salt until the desired amount has collected on the glass.

Measure the tequila, Cointreau, and lemon or lime juice into a 16-ounce cocktail shaker glass full of ice. Place a stainless steel cocktail shaker over the glass, tapping the top to create a seal. Shake vigorously for about 5 seconds and pour into the salt-rimmed glass.

Margarita Tip It is a common misconception that margaritas were invented to cool off the heat of chiles in Mexican food. Not so—in fact, a lot of Mexican food isn't hot at all. On the other hand, since most New Mexican, modern Southwestern, and Tex-Mex food is *picante*, perhaps the margarita does make a nice alternative to beer when you're eating our wonderful regional fare.

Tequila Tidbit Blue agave "leaves" are shaped rather like swords, with a sharp tip. They are called **pencas** in Mexico. These "leaves" are removed before the heart of the plant is processed to make tequila.

THE SANTIAGO MARGARITA
Makes 1 margarita

This margarita was inspired by a longtime Maria's patron named James (Santiago translates as St. James in English) who wanted to improve on an existing margarita, The Rafael (see page 34). James suggested that we substitute Herradura Silver Natural 100-percent blue agave tequila for the Cuervo Gold, and whaddya know, he helped us create one of the smoothest and most elegant margaritas around.

> 1 lemon or lime wedge
> Saucer of kosher salt (about ¼-inch deep)
> 1¼ ounces Herradura Silver Natural tequila
> 1 ounce Cointreau
> 1½ ounces freshly squeezed lemon or lime juice
> Ice

Run the lemon or lime wedge around the rim of a hurricane-style margarita glass. Dip the rim of the glass into the saucer of salt, rotating the rim in the salt until the desired amount has collected on the glass.

Measure the tequila, Cointreau, and lemon or lime juice into a 16-ounce cocktail shaker glass full of ice. Place a stainless steel cocktail shaker over the glass, tapping the top to create a seal. Shake vigorously for about 5 seconds and pour into the salt-rimmed glass.

Tequila Tidbit **The major tequila producers each own several million agave plants, and a few grow them organically. Herradura is one of these ecology-friendly producers.**

THE HERRADURA GOLD MARGARITA

Makes 1 margarita

Back when tequila in the United States was exclusive to the Southwest because the East Coast hadn't yet discovered it, tequila aficionados would brag about the smooth, outstanding flavor of Herradura Gold. These folks would never use this wonderful nectar in a margarita— "Sorry," they'd say, "this is sippin' stuff." Well, we think this "sippin' stuff" makes an awesome margarita. Herradura recently changed their label to read "reposado" instead of "gold" to keep up with the market of more knowledgeable consumers.

> 1 lemon or lime wedge
> Saucer of kosher salt (about ¼-inch deep)
> 1¼ ounces Herradura reposado natural 100-percent
>   agave tequila
> 1 ounce Cointreau
> 1½ ounces freshly squeezed lemon or lime juice
> Ice

Run the lemon or lime wedge around the rim of a hurricane-style margarita glass. Dip the rim of the glass into the saucer of salt, rotating the rim in the salt until the desired amount has collected on the glass.

Measure the tequila, Cointreau, and lemon or lime juice into a 16-ounce cocktail shaker glass full of ice. Place a stainless steel cocktail shaker over the glass, tapping the top to create a seal. Shake vigorously for about 5 seconds and pour into the salt-rimmed glass.

Margarita Tip The glasses we use for our real margaritas are made by the Libbey Glass Company. The hurricane-style, 13¼-ounce "rocks" glasses are called Poco Grande II. The saucer-type glasses are Coupette/ Margarita. They can be ordered from a good kitchen store or any Libbey Glass dealer.

Tequila Tidbit The blue agave flavor of Herradura reposado natural is enhanced by aging in oak barrels, which imparts a light golden hue to the tequila. Herradura Silver Natural is a premium tequila, produced from 100-percent blue agave, with no aging.

THE HERRADURA AÑEJO MARGARITA

Makes 1 margarita

Herradura was the first 100-percent blue agave tequila to be imported into the United States and effectively marketed, which gave it a head start on other superpremium brands. This is probably the main reason why it is just about the best known of the superpremium tequilas available; some tequila fans would say that this is the finest of them all. The rich, flavorful taste of Herradura añejo tequila is enhanced by 2 full years of aging.

> 1 lemon or lime wedge
> Saucer of kosher salt (about ¼-inch deep)
> 1¼ ounces Herradura añejo tequila
> 1 ounce Cointreau
> 1½ ounces freshly squeezed lemon or lime juice
> Ice

Run the lemon or lime wedge around the rim of a hurricane-style margarita glass. Dip the rim of the glass into the saucer of salt, rotating the rim in the salt until the desired amount has collected on the glass.

Measure the tequila, Cointreau, and lemon or lime juice into a 16-ounce cocktail shaker glass full of ice. Place a stainless steel cocktail shaker over the glass, tapping the top to create a seal. Shake vigorously for about 5 seconds and pour into the salt-rimmed glass.

Tequila Tidbit **The blue agave plant is a succulent and not a cactus, as some people would have you believe. It is kin to the aloe vera plant, which it resembles on a bigger scale. (Maybe that explains why 100-percent agave tequila is so smooth!)**

El Tesoro

El Tesoro tequilas are arguably the finest tequilas of all. They are handmade from estate-grown agave only, and every piña is harvested when it is individually mature, rather than when most of the agave in one field or another are ready. The piñas are then cut, roasted in steam ovens for 2 days, and squeezed with a huge millstone to extract the sweetness. The juice is then transferred by hand to vats, fermented, then double-distilled to the exact proof desired. El Tesoro is literally fermented to proof; the aguamiel, or sweet agave juice, is poured into fermenting vats with the exact amount of yeast to begin the fermentation process. It is one of the most flavorful of all tequilas because nothing else is added. All this makes El Tesoro one of the purest forms of alcoholic beverage made today.

THE ELIZABETH II MARGARITA

Makes 1 margarita

One of Maria's cocktail waitresses, Elizabeth, was explaining to a customer that when a margarita was mixed using the premium El Tesoro tequila and Grand Marnier, the latter dominated the tequila, while a margarita made with El Tesoro and Cointreau allowed the flavor to emerge more fully. The customer was a Grand Marnier lover, however, and asked Elizabeth if the bartender would be willing to mix a margarita using El Tesoro, a half measure of Grand Marnier, and a half measure of Cointreau. It proved to be a winning combination, and the name Elizabeth II stuck, referring to one Elizabeth and two orange liqueurs. For as long as I can remember, anyone who has ordered an Elizabeth II once has ordered it again.

> 1 lemon or lime wedge
> Saucer of kosher salt (about ¼-inch deep)
> 1¼ ounces El Tesoro 100-percent blue agave plata tequila
> ½ ounce Grand Marnier
> ½ ounce Cointreau
> 1½ ounces freshly squeezed lemon or lime juice
> Ice

Run the lemon or lime wedge around the rim of a hurricane-style margarita glass. Dip the rim of the glass into the saucer of salt, rotating the rim in the salt until the desired amount has collected on the glass.

Measure the tequila, Grand Marnier, Cointreau, and lemon or lime juice into a 16-ounce cocktail shaker glass full of ice. Place a stainless steel cocktail shaker over the glass, tapping the top to create a seal. Shake vigorously for about 5 seconds and pour into the salt-rimmed glass.

Tequila Tidbit All El Tesoro tequilas are 100-percent blue agave, handmade, and double-distilled at precisely the right time to produce an 80-proof liquor (40 percent alcohol by volume). Most other distilled spirits either have distilled water added to lower the proof or alcohol added to raise the proof.

MARIA'S FAMOUS LA ULTIMA MARGARITA

Makes 1 margarita

This is one of the very first superpremium margaritas to be marketed in the world. Up until this particular margarita, most tequila connoisseurs would only drink their precious 100-percent superpremium nectar straight. There should be no substituting any of the ingredients in this margarita. Taste them all together and I'm confident that you will find it will live up to its name, "The Ultimate Margarita."

> 1 lemon or lime wedge
> Saucer of kosher salt (about ¼-inch deep)
> 1¼ ounces El Tesoro 100-percent blue agave plata tequila
> 1 ounce Cointreau
> 1½ ounces freshly squeezed lemon or lime juice
> Ice

Run the lemon or lime wedge around the rim of a hurricane-style margarita glass. Dip the rim of the glass into the saucer of salt, rotating the rim in the salt until the desired amount has collected on the glass.

Measure the tequila, Cointreau, and lemon or lime juice into a 16-ounce cocktail shaker glass full of ice. Place a stainless steel cocktail shaker over the glass, tapping the top to create a seal. Shake vigorously for about 5 seconds and pour into the salt-rimmed glass.

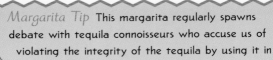

Margarita Tip This margarita regularly spawns debate with tequila connoisseurs who accuse us of violating the integrity of the tequila by using it in a margarita. So you be the judge. Sip a little El Tesoro plata on its own. Then make up this margarita and taste it. Which is more pleasant? I think the margarita is so much more enjoyable than even the best tequila. (I rarely drink tequila straight anymore.)

Tequila Tidbit Maria's pours more El Tesoro tequila than any other restaurant or bar in America. Our Maria's Famous La Ultima Margarita is largely responsible for this.

THE GRAND PLATINUM MARGARITA

Makes 1 margarita

This margarita is made with two of the most expensive distilled spirits available: 100-percent blue agave El Tesoro plata (silver) tequila and Grand Marnier. You do get what you pay for, though. Here is a world-class cocktail that is probably one of the purest, most natural concoctions you can enjoy. El Tesoro is handmade and double-distilled to proof, while Grand Marnier is triple-distilled from exotic oranges and peels with premium cognac added. And of course, the lemon juice is freshly squeezed from one of nature's most efficient and remarkable containers.

> 1 lemon or lime wedge
> Saucer of kosher salt (about ¼-inch deep)
> 1¼ ounces El Tesoro 100-percent blue agave plata
>   tequila
> 1 ounce Grand Marnier
> 1½ ounces freshly squeezed lemon or lime juice
> Ice

Run the lemon or lime wedge around the rim of a hurricane-style margarita glass. Dip the rim of the glass into the saucer of salt, rotating the rim in the salt until the desired amount has collected on the glass.

Measure the tequila, Grand Marnier, and lemon or lime juice into a 16-ounce cocktail shaker glass full of ice. Place a stainless steel cocktail shaker over the glass, tapping the top to create a seal. Shake vigorously for about 5 seconds and pour into the salt-rimmed glass.

Tequila Tidbit A few tequila makers still grow, harvest, cook, and distill their own agave and wouldn't think of using any other agave. One such tequila is El Tesoro de Don Felipe (we refer to this brand as simply "El Tesoro"), from the highlands of Jalisco in the Arandas area of Mexico. There, Don Felipe and his family select only the agave piñas that have reached maturity and harvest them for their estate-grown 100-percent agave tequila. The advantage: total quality control, from planting to cultivating to harvesting to distilling and bottling (not unlike estate-grown and -bottled Bordeaux in France).

THE MOONGLOW MARGARITA

Makes 1 margarita

El Tesoro de Don Felipe tequila was one of the first 100-percent agave superpremium tequilas to be imported into the United States, after the longstanding reign of Herradura, which was the first such tequila on American shelves. For many years, El Tesoro was available only in blanco and añejo, and eager El Tesoro fans waited and waited for the reposado to be imported. Finally it was. We immediately mixed it with Cointreau and lemon juice and couldn't help but notice the color of the margarita was that of moonglow—hence the name. Mix it up and you'll agree.

> 1 lemon or lime wedge
> Saucer of kosher salt (about ¼-inch deep)
> 1¼ ounces El Tesoro reposado tequila
> 1 ounce Cointreau
> 1½ ounces freshly squeezed lemon or lime juice
> Ice

Run the lemon or lime wedge around the rim of a hurricane-style margarita glass. Dip the rim of the glass into the saucer of salt, rotating the rim in the salt until the desired amount has collected on the glass.

Measure the tequila, Cointreau, and lemon or lime juice into a 16-ounce cocktail shaker glass full of ice. Place a stainless steel cocktail shaker over the glass, tapping the top to create a seal. Shake vigorously for about 5 seconds and pour into the salt-rimmed glass.

Margarita Tip Invite some friends over and compare the different flavors you are able to create by using a single tequila (such as El Tesoro) and interchanging the Cointreau with Grand Marnier or triple sec. You can also experiment with substituting fresh lime juice for the lemon juice.

Tequila Tidbit The silicate-based volcanic soil around Tequila in the state of Jalisco (which produces by far the most tequila) is ideal for growing the blue agave plant.

THE GRAND MOONGLOW MARGARITA

Makes 1 margarita

The arrival of the reposado 100-percent agave tequila from El Tesoro was such a treat and it made such a delightful visual and taste experience with the Cointreau, we had to try it with Grand Marnier. The result: Grand! The moonglow coloring was a bit deeper with the Grand Marnier and the taste was outstanding—just a bit stronger than with the Cointreau. The hint of the cognac used in the Grand Marnier makes our Grand Moonglow a favorite at Maria's!

- 1 lemon or lime wedge
- Saucer of kosher salt (about ¼-inch deep)
- 1¼ ounces El Tesoro reposado tequila
- 1 ounce Grand Marnier
- 1½ ounces freshly squeezed lemon or lime juice
- Ice

Run the lemon or lime wedge around the rim of a hurricane-style margarita glass. Dip the rim of the glass into the saucer of salt, rotating the rim in the salt until the desired amount has collected on the glass.

Measure the tequila, Grand Marnier, and lemon or lime juice into a 16-ounce cocktail shaker glass full of ice. Place a stainless steel cocktail shaker over the glass, tapping the top to create a seal. Shake vigorously for about 5 seconds and pour into the salt-rimmed glass.

Tequila Tidbit The mature blue agave plant is called the **madre** (mother plant) by tequila growers. The young plants that spring from the madre's roots are called **hijuelos**, or little children. These offspring are left to grow next to the mother plant for 4 or 5 years before they are replanted.

EL BAILE DEL SOL MARGARITA
Makes 1 margarita

This margarita is a salute to our friend—the fellow who says all those kind things about Maria's in the foreword of this book—The Sundance Kid, Robert Redford. This exceptional margarita uses ¾-ounce of El Tesoro 100-percent agave añejo tequila blended with the same amount of Chinaco 100-percent agave añejo tequila. They dance together with the sunshine of Cointreau and freshly squeezed lemon juice to create the fantastic margarita named "El Baile del Sol," which translates to "The Sundance"!

> 1 lemon or lime wedge
> Saucer of kosher salt (about ¼-inch deep)
> ¾ ounce El Tesoro 100-percent agave añejo tequila
> ¾ ounce Chinaco 100-percent agave añejo tequila
> 1 ounce Cointreau
> 1½ ounces freshly squeezed lemon or lime juice
> Ice

Run the lemon or lime wedge around the rim of a hurricane-style margarita glass. Dip the rim of the glass into the saucer of salt, rotating the rim in the salt until the desired amount has collected on the glass.

Measure the tequilas, Cointreau, and lemon or lime juice into a 16-ounce cocktail shaker glass full of ice. Place a stainless steel cocktail shaker over the glass, tapping the top to create a seal. Shake vigorously for about 5 seconds and pour into the salt-rimmed glass.

Margarita Tip Because you are going to be the Margarita Maven in your circle of friends, invest in a small, 3-pound box of kosher salt. This will last awhile and is sure to really impress your pals.

Tequila Tidbit If you travel to Mexico and despair when you cannot find El Tesoro anywhere on the shelves, take heart! This family of tequilas is called Tapatio south of the border. Other tequila makers also market their products under different brand names at home and abroad.

THE GRAND TREASURE MARGARITA
Makes 1 margarita

Tequila lovers who have tried most of the 100-percent blue agave tequilas on the market generally have their own preferred "sipping" tequila. El Tesoro muy añejo ("very aged") tequila is certainly a contender for the title of Best Tequila in the World (let's not pull any punches). This is a tequila to enjoy in a brandy snifter after dinner. Try it some time—you'll think you're sipping a fine cognac. This margarita combines muy añejo tequila with Grand Marnier, which is popular with those who enjoy a heavier alcohol taste rather than the subtle agave flavor of silver tequilas.

> 1 lemon or lime wedge
> Saucer of kosher salt (about ¼-inch deep)
> 1¼ ounces El Tesoro 100-percent blue agave añejo
>   tequila
> 1 ounce Grand Marnier
> 1½ ounces freshly squeezed lemon or lime juice
> Ice

Run the lemon or lime wedge around the rim of a hurricane-style margarita glass. Dip the rim of the glass into the saucer of salt, rotating the rim in the salt until the desired amount has collected on the glass.

Measure the tequila, Grand Marnier, and lemon or lime juice into a 16-ounce cocktail shaker glass full of ice. Place a stainless steel cocktail shaker over the glass, tapping the top to create a seal. Shake vigorously for about 5 seconds and pour into the salt-rimmed glass.

Margarita Tip At Maria's we think tequila should be drunk in margaritas, so we strongly discourage shots and slammers—we believe folks have a tendency to over-indulge when drinking tequila this way. We want our guests to drink liquor because they like it, not because they want to get drunk.

Tequila Tidbit Even though the golden El Tesoro muy añejo tequila is handmade, double-distilled to proof, and then carefully aged in oak barrels for more than 2 years, I prefer the "fresh" newly distilled El Tesoro plata (silver). The aging process seems to cause the tequila to lose the deep agave flavor that is unique to superpremium 100-percent blue agave tequila.

LA MARGARITA DEL JOVEN ESTEBAN

Makes 1 margarita

We named this margarita after one of Maria's longtime waiters, Steve Young (joven means "young"), who couldn't understand why we didn't have a margarita on our list that combined the El Tesoro muy añejo and Cointreau. After all, we had both El Tesoro Plata and El Tesoro añejo margaritas mixed with Cointreau. Steve conned us into believing that his customers insisted on El Tesoro muy añejo and Cointreau margaritas (which they did—after a little coaching from Steve). Since we believe that the customer is always right, and because we heard rave reviews from the customers drinking this concoction, we decided to add it to our Real Margaritas List and name it after Steve.

I lemon or lime wedge
Saucer of kosher salt (about ¼-inch deep)
1¼ ounces El Tesoro 100-percent blue agave añejo
    tequila
1 ounce Cointreau
1½ ounces freshly squeezed lemon or lime juice
Ice

Run the lemon or lime wedge around the rim of a hurricane-style margarita glass. Dip the rim of the glass into the saucer of salt, rotating the rim in the salt until the desired amount has collected on the glass.

Measure the tequila, Cointreau, and lemon or lime juice into a 16-ounce cocktail shaker glass full of ice. Place a stainless steel cocktail shaker over the glass, tapping the top to create a seal. Shake vigorously for about 5 seconds and pour into the salt-rimmed glass.

Tequila Tidbit **Many tequila producers will tell you that their tequila is unique because of their water supply, and that it is the water used in the distilling process that makes all the difference to flavor and quality. Many producers boast that their own private wells produce the best water.**

LA MARGARITA DE PARADISO
Makes 1 margarita

Yes, my friends, this is the $40 margarita. The first thing people ask about this drink is, "Is it really worth that much?" Our reply: "Definitely." It's made with one of the finest tequilas ever made, Paradiso by El Tesoro. The company ages freshly distilled 100-percent agave tequila in several different styles of cognac oak barrels that are imported from the Cognac region of France. Another import by El Tesoro is Alain Royer, the master cognac blender, who then weaves his magic to create the liquid nectar called Paradiso. Not wishing to stop there, we have added the 150th Anniversary Cuvee Speciale Grand Marnier and lemon juice to create the most awesome margarita ever.

1 lemon or lime wedge
Saucer of kosher salt (about ¼-inch deep)
1¼ ounces El Tesoro Paradiso 100-percent agave añejo
    tequila
1 ounce 150th Anniversary Cuvee Speciale
    Centcinquantenaire Grand Marnier
1½ ounces freshly squeezed lemon or lime juice
Ice

Run the lemon or lime wedge around the rim of a hurricane-style margarita glass. Dip the rim of the glass into the saucer of salt, rotating the rim in the salt until the desired amount has collected on the glass.

Measure the tequila, Grand Marnier, and lemon or lime juice into a 16-ounce cocktail shaker glass full of ice. Place a stainless steel cocktail shaker over the glass, tapping the top to create a seal. Shake vigorously for about 5 seconds and pour into the salt-rimmed glass.

Tequila Tidbit The tequila and Grand Marnier used in this cocktail are very expensive, and we advise keeping them together—do not substitute either one. Paradiso served on its own in a brandy snifter will rival the finest cognac.

Porfidio

Todhunter Imports, Ltd., responsible for bringing Porfidio tequila into the United States, has taken a page out of the Absolut vodka book. They are second to none when it comes to designer bottles for their tequila, and with all due respect, the tequila that they put into these bottles is really very good. They use several different distillers to bottle their 100-percent agave tequilas, so if you really care, look at the NOM number on each bottle and it will tell you where it was produced.

Porfidio features a silver tequila, a triple-distilled tequila (see The Porfidio Triple-Triple Margarita on page 70), a reposado (bottled in a handsome royal blue ceramic bottle with a little bitty cork), their single-barrel añejo, and their Barrique limited edition, which is aged in select fresh Limousin oak casks (it retails for about $400 a bottle). Besides paying for the bottle, don't be misled by the saguaro cactus in the bottom of the single-barrel añejo . . . remember, tequila comes from the blue agave plant, which is not a cactus. Other than that small quibble, this is a great product—we take our hats off to their marketing department!

THE PORFIDIO DE PLATA MARGARITA
Makes 1 margarita

This recipe uses the 100-percent agave Limited Edition Silver tequila from Porfidio, their basic product. It produces a clean, full-of-agave-flavor margarita when we mix it with Cointreau and freshly squeezed lemon juice.

> 1 lemon or lime wedge
> Saucer of kosher salt (about ¼-inch deep)
> 1¼ ounces Porfidio 100-percent agave silver tequila
> 1 ounce Cointreau
> 1½ ounces freshly squeezed lemon or lime juice
> Ice

Run the lemon or lime wedge around the rim of a hurricane-style margarita glass. Dip the rim of the glass into the saucer of salt, rotating the rim in the salt until the desired amount has collected on the glass.

Measure the tequila, Cointreau, and lemon or lime juice into a 16-ounce cocktail shaker glass full of ice. Place a stainless steel cocktail shaker over the glass, tapping the top to create a seal. Shake vigorously for about 5 seconds and pour into the salt-rimmed glass.

Tequila Tidbit Used oak barrels are favored for aging tequila because they tend to impact the liquor less. Previous use (often, for aging bourbon) has already extracted some of the wood color and flavor, leaving the tequila purer.

THE PORFIDIO TRIPLE-TRIPLE MARGARITA

Makes 1 margarita

The Mexican government regulates tequila production more than most other products, and one of the regulations imposed in the distilling of tequila is that it be distilled twice. Porfidio has gone one step further by triple-distilling this 100-percent agave plata tequila. We think that mixing it with the triple-distilled Cointreau and freshly squeezed lemon juice results in the purest cocktail ever created. . . . The Triple-Triple!

1 lemon or lime wedge
Saucer of kosher salt (about ¼-inch deep)
1¼ ounces Porfidio 100-percent agave silver tequila
1 ounce Cointreau
1½ ounces freshly squeezed lemon or lime juice
Ice

Run the lemon or lime wedge around the rim of a hurricane-style margarita glass. Dip the rim of the glass into the saucer of salt, rotating the rim in the salt until the desired amount has collected on the glass.

Measure the tequila, Cointreau, and lemon or lime juice into a 16-ounce cocktail shaker glass full of ice. Place a stainless steel cocktail shaker over the glass, tapping the top to create a seal. Shake vigorously for about 5 seconds and pour into the salt-rimmed glass.

Margarita Tip If you hold a tequila-tasting party, code the glasses for a blind tasting and keep score—it's always a good idea to keep notes for future reference. Most importantly, appoint designated drivers in advance if necessary.

Tequila Tidbit The label for this tequila claims, "Porfidio plata achieves a truly rare distinction of 100% agave fermentation and extra refinement in a three distillation process, providing extra clarity and a totally new discovery in taste." We agree!

70

THE PORFIDIO REPOSADO
MARGARITA
Makes 1 margarita

With the success of their marketing in distinctively shaped, handblown glass bottles, the Porfidio folks ventured into uncharted waters with the recent introduction of their 100-percent agave reposado tequila. Porfidio reposado is packaged in a limited edition royal blue ceramic bottle with a little narrow neck capped by a tiny cork. The bottle will definitely catch your eye, and the tequila will definitely catch your palate. We mixed it with Cointreau and freshly squeezed lemon juice to create the Porfidio Reposado margarita—so simple, yet such a delicious and delightful drink.

> 1 lemon or lime wedge
> Saucer of kosher salt (about ¼-inch deep)
> 1¼ ounces Porfidio 100-percent agave reposado tequila
> 1 ounce Cointreau
> 1½ ounces freshly squeezed lemon or lime juice
> Ice

Run the lemon or lime wedge around the rim of a hurricane-style margarita glass. Dip the rim of the glass into the saucer of salt, rotating the rim in the salt until the desired amount has collected on the glass.

Measure the tequila, Cointreau, and lemon or lime juice into a 16-ounce cocktail shaker glass full of ice. Place a stainless steel cocktail shaker over the glass, tapping the top to create a seal. Shake vigorously for about 5 seconds and pour into the salt-rimmed glass.

Tequila Tidbit While tequila is made exclusively from the blue agave, other agaves are processed to make alcoholic beverages. In addition to mezcal, **bacanora** is produced in the northern state of Sonora, **raicillo** is produced in Jalisco, and **comiteca** is another regional variation on the same theme. With the exception of mezcal, these local liquors are only found in Mexico and are not exported.

THE PORFIDIO AÑEJO MARGARITA
Makes 1 margarita

Porfidio uses several different distillers in Jalisco to produce their out-standing line of tequilas. According to the NOM on their añejo bottle, they use Jesus Reyes (see page 109) to produce and age their 100 percent agave añejo tequila. Porfidio añejo is aged on oak for at least 2 years, which provides a distinctive flavor to this fine product. We have experimented with Porfidio añejo using Grand Marnier and feel that the cognac in the Grand Marnier overwhelmed the delicate flavors of the tequila. Then we tried Cointreau and—wow! Mix this one up for a terrific taste treat!

> 1 lemon or lime wedge
> Saucer of kosher salt (about ¼-inch deep)
> 1¼ ounces Porfidio 100-percent agave añejo tequila
> 1 ounce Cointreau
> 1½ ounces freshly squeezed lemon or lime juice
> Ice

Run the lemon or lime wedge around the rim of a hurricane-style margarita glass. Dip the rim of the glass into the saucer of salt, rotating the rim in the salt until the desired amount has collected on the glass.

Measure the tequila, Cointreau, and lemon or lime juice into a 16-ounce cocktail shaker glass full of ice. Place a stainless steel cocktail shaker over the glass, tapping the top to create a seal. Shake vigorously for about 5 seconds and pour into the salt-rimmed glass.

Margarita Tip When you serve margaritas using plastic glasses, use table salt instead of kosher salt because it sticks much better to the plastic. There's something about the coarser texture of kosher salt that just hates plastic!

Tequila Tidbit Until the 1930s, all tequila was 100-percent blue agave. Because of increasing demand, the producers began mixing in cane sugar, thus introducing the 51-percent agave tequilas that dominate the market today.

THE PORFIDIO SINGLE BARREL PERFECTO MARGARITA

Makes 1 margarita

This wonderful margarita features Porfidio 100-percent agave añejo single-barrel tequila. This is the handblown bottle with the glass saguaro cactus inside. Tequila is not made from cactus—the Weber blue agave is a succulent, so the attractive packaging is a little misleading. This is a grand tequila, but its price is inflated because you are paying for the unique bottle.

> 1 lemon or lime wedge
> Saucer of kosher salt (about ¼-inch deep)
> 1¼ ounces Porfidio single-barrel 100-percent agave
>   añejo tequila
> 1 ounce Cointreau
> 1½ ounces freshly squeezed lemon or lime juice
> Ice

Run the lemon or lime wedge around the rim of a hurricane-style margarita glass. Dip the rim of the glass into the saucer of salt, rotating the rim in the salt until the desired amount has collected on the glass.

Measure the tequila, Cointreau, and lemon or lime juice into a 16-ounce cocktail shaker glass full of ice. Place a stainless steel cocktail shaker over the glass, tapping the top to create a seal. Shake vigorously for about 5 seconds and pour into the salt-rimmed glass.

Tequila Tidbit Jimmy Buffett's song "Margarita-ville" did much to spur awareness of margaritas and contribute to their popularity. The song became the unofficial anthem for the laid-back town of Key West in Florida, Jimmy Buffet's home.

Patrón

Patrón is one of the great original entries into the U.S. superpremium 100-percent blue agave market. You know you're in for a treat the minute you see the unique hand-blown reusable decanter-type bottle, complete with a cork-lined handblown glass stopper. On the other hand, there's no free lunch, as they say, and though this is an outstanding tequila, Patrón is generally a little higher priced than others of comparable quality, almost certainly because of its superior packaging. If you have use for the decanter, Patrón is a particular bargain; if not, you will be paying for it anyway—you be the judge.

LA MARGARITA DE LA PATRÓNA

Makes 1 margarita

This margarita is made with Patrón Silver—a 100-percent blue agave tequila from the highlands of Jalisco (an area that is increasingly touted by tequila experts as the prime agave-growing region of Mexico). Patrón in Spanish means "boss," and la patróna is the feminine version, or loosely translated, "boss lady"—so here we present "the boss lady's margarita."

> 1 lemon or lime wedge
> Saucer of kosher salt (about ¼-inch deep)
> 1¼ ounces Patrón 100-percent blue agave silver tequila
> 1 ounce Cointreau
> 1½ ounces freshly squeezed lemon or lime juice
> Ice

Run the lemon or lime wedge around the rim of a hurricane-style margarita glass. Dip the rim of the glass into the saucer of salt, rotating the rim in the salt until the desired amount has collected on the glass.

Measure the tequila, Cointreau, and lemon or lime juice into a 16-ounce cocktail shaker glass full of ice. Place a stainless steel cocktail shaker over the glass, tapping the top to create a seal. Shake vigorously for about 5 seconds and pour into the salt-rimmed glass.

Tequila Tidbit By the early 1990s, tequila had become the tenth-bestselling spirit in the United States, at 5.1 million cases (vodka is the market leader). Tequila is also the fastest-growing spirit in terms of sales, largely because of the ever-increasing popularity of margaritas.

THE DON ROBERTO MARGARITA
Makes 1 margarita

This margarita is named for Bob Noyes, a former partner of ours at Maria's, both because he is a patrón—*one of the bosses*—and because this is his favorite margarita. It features Patrón añejo tequila, which like the silver version (page 75) is bottled in handblown glass decanter-type bottles.

> 1 lemon or lime wedge
> Saucer of kosher salt (about ¼-inch deep)
> 1¼ ounces Patrón 100-percent blue agave añejo tequila
> 1 ounce Cointreau
> 1½ ounces freshly squeezed lemon or lime juice
> Ice

Run the lemon or lime wedge around the rim of a hurricane-style margarita glass. Dip the rim of the glass into the saucer of salt, rotating the rim in the salt until the desired amount has collected on the glass.

Measure the tequila, Cointreau, and lemon or lime juice into a 16-ounce cocktail shaker glass full of ice. Place a stainless steel cocktail shaker over the glass, tapping the top to create a seal. Shake vigorously for about 5 seconds and pour into the salt-rimmed glass.

Margarita Tip Since the word "tequila" refers to the town situated in the volcanic lava hills of the Jalisco region, we decided to experiment with a Volcano Margarita, made with dry ice (to create the volcano smoke) and Tabasco (for the heat). All the other ingredients—tequila, triple sec, and lemon juice—were as usual. It was awful. The moral of this tale is that you can experiment all you want, but not everything you try to make into a margarita is going to be a true delight.

Tequila Tidbit Blue agave plants grown for making tequila are planted about 3 feet apart, in rows. The mature plants reach 6 to 8 feet.

LA MARGARITA DE LA DOÑA HELEN

Makes 1 margarita

When a tequila as popular as Patrón introduces a new product, it's an exciting event for a barkeep who offers almost 100 different margaritas. That was the case when Patrón began importing its 100-percent agave reposado. With several margaritas already on the list made with Patrón silver and añejo tequilas, we quickly began the mixing and tasting (tough job, but somebody has to do it). The resulting margarita using Patrón reposado and Cointreau was so smooth and elegant that we decided to name it in honor of the employee who has been with Maria's almost 30 years, Helen Maestas. Want an extra-smooth margarita? Try this one!

> 1 lemon or lime wedge
> Saucer of kosher salt (about ¼-inch deep)
> 1¼ ounces Patrón 100-percent agave reposado tequila
> 1 ounce Cointreau
> 1½ ounces freshly squeezed lemon or lime juice
> Ice

Run the lemon or lime wedge around the rim of a hurricane-style margarita glass. Dip the rim of the glass into the saucer of salt, rotating the rim in the salt until the desired amount has collected on the glass.

Measure the tequila, Cointreau, and lemon or lime juice into a 16-ounce cocktail shaker glass full of ice. Place a stainless steel cocktail shaker over the glass, tapping the top to create a seal. Shake vigorously for about 5 seconds and pour into the salt-rimmed glass.

Tequila Tidbit All Patrón tequila is made with large stone milling wheels that squeeze all the juices from the steam-cooked agave piñas. The fermentation process includes the pressed piña fibers, which the manufacturer claims help impart the unique flavor and smoothness. The fermented liquid is then double-distilled and hand-bottled. The quality of this particular tequila as well as the unique packaging make this one of our favorite gifts for housewarmings, holidays, or just special friends.

Centinela

Centinela is another handmade 100-percent blue agave tequila, and it's produced and bottled at the distillery in the mountains near Arandas, in the state of Jalisco. Centinela has been produced for more than one hundred years and is available in four forms: plata (or blanco) white tequila; reposado, which is aged for 3 months; añejo, which is aged for 1 year; and añejo tres años, their top-of-the-line tequila, which is aged for 3 years.

THE CENTINELA REPOSADO MARGARITA

Makes 1 margarita

Centinela is distributed in the United States by El Dorado Importers, based in Santa Rosa, New Mexico. We reckon it is one of the best values of all the superpremium tequilas being imported to the United States.

> 1 lemon or lime wedge
> Saucer of kosher salt (about ¼-inch deep)
> 1¼ ounces Centinela 100-percent blue agave reposado tequila
> 1 ounce Cointreau
> 1½ ounces freshly squeezed lemon or lime juice
> Ice

Run the lemon or lime wedge around the rim of a hurricane-style margarita glass. Dip the rim of the glass into the saucer of salt, rotating the rim in the salt until the desired amount has collected on the glass.

Measure the tequila, Cointreau, and lemon or lime juice into a 16-ounce cocktail shaker glass full of ice. Place a stainless steel cocktail shaker over the glass, tapping the top to create a seal. Shake vigorously for about 5 seconds and pour into the salt-rimmed glass.

Tequila Tidbit Mezcal is not tequila. We can call mezcal a cousin to tequila because it is generally made from the same agave plant. However, mezcal is not usually double-distilled and, unlike tequila, is not subject to any governmental regulations.

THE SILVER SENTINEL MARGARITA
Makes 1 margarita

Centinela is from the same region as El Tesoro (same climate and same soil conditions) and can be favorably compared with any 100-percent blue agave tequila. The plata Centinela used in this margarita is smooth, with a dry-sweet taste.

> 1 lemon or lime wedge
> Saucer of kosher salt (about ¼-inch deep)
> 1¼ ounces Centinela 100-percent blue agave blanco tequila
> 1 ounce Cointreau
> 1½ ounces freshly squeezed lemon or lime juice
> Ice

Run the lemon or lime wedge around the rim of a hurricane-style margarita glass. Dip the rim of the glass into the saucer of salt, rotating the rim in the salt until the desired amount has collected on the glass.

Measure the tequila, Cointreau, and lemon or lime juice into a 16-ounce cocktail shaker glass full of ice. Place a stainless steel cocktail shaker over the glass, tapping the top to create a seal. Shake vigorously for about 5 seconds and pour into the salt-rimmed glass.

Margarita Tip Here's another fun taste test. Splurge on a bottle of each of the different types of tequila made by one producer, such as Centinela. Make margaritas using identical ingredients except for the different forms of the one brand of tequila and compare notes.

Tequila Tidbit The ancient Mexican Indian cultures handled drunkenness (usually caused by drinking too much pulque) by shaving the perpetrator's head—the sign of disgrace—for the first offense. The punishment for a second offense was a little more harsh—death!

THE BLUE ANGEL MARGARITA
Makes 1 margarita

Way back when, some enterprising individual decided to make a blue margarita, and the only obvious way to do that was to use blue curaçao instead of triple sec. Blue curaçao is an orange liqueur made from the juice and peel of Curaçao oranges with blue food coloring added. This makes a fun cocktail, and the Blue Angel Margarita is one of the few drinks at Maria's that contains any artificial ingredients.

    1 lemon or lime wedge
    Saucer of kosher salt (about ¼-inch deep)
    1¼ ounces Centinela 100-percent blue agave blanco
        tequila
    1 ounce Bols blue curaçao (or add blue food coloring to
        triple sec)
    1½ ounces freshly squeezed lemon or lime juice
    Ice

Run the lemon or lime wedge around the rim of a hurricane-style margarita glass. Dip the rim of the glass into the saucer of salt, rotating the rim in the salt until the desired amount has collected on the glass. For even more fun, use colored salt on this one.

Measure the tequila, blue curaçao, and lemon or lime juice into a 16-ounce cocktail shaker glass full of ice. Place a stainless steel cocktail shaker over the glass, tapping the top to create a seal. Shake vigorously for about 5 seconds and pour into the salt-rimmed glass.

Tequila Tidbit Blue agave is so called because of the bluish hues that the fields of the plants give as they undulate along the hillsides of the Sierra Madre range. The juices of these plants are not, as some suppose, blue—in fact, once they have been fermented and double-distilled into tequila, they are crystal clear.

THE HUNDRED GRAND MARGARITA

Makes 1 margarita

When we taste-tested this margarita using Centinela's añejo tequila, it was so smooth and the tequila flavor was so alive that we thought we had used Cointreau instead of Grand Marnier. This is a reflection of the fine taste of this particular tequila and backs our contention that Centinela añejo is one of the best tequilas available in the United States.

- 1 lemon or lime wedge
- Saucer of kosher salt (about ¼-inch deep)
- 1¼ ounces Centinela 100-percent blue agave añejo tequila
- 1 ounce Grand Marnier
- 1½ ounces freshly squeezed lemon or lime juice
- Ice

Run the lemon or lime wedge around the rim of a hurricane-style margarita glass. Dip the rim of the glass into the saucer of salt, rotating the rim in the salt until the desired amount has collected on the glass.

Measure the tequila, Grand Marnier, and lemon or lime juice into a 16-ounce cocktail shaker glass full of ice. Place a stainless steel cocktail shaker over the glass, tapping the top to create a seal. Shake vigorously for about 5 seconds and pour into the salt-rimmed glass.

Margarita Tip As mentioned earlier, Grand Marnier often tends to overwhelm the flavor of the tequila in a margarita. However, when you use Grand Marnier with the right tequila—like Centinela's añejo—there is no better margarita in the world.

Tequila Tidbit When visiting Mexico, you may hear the agave plant referred to as maguey. It is still the same plant, the Agave tequilana Weber, blue variety. "Maguey" is what the Spanish explorers called agave when they first came into the tequila country.

THE CENTINELA AÑEJO
MARGARITA
Makes 1 margarita

Just as the smooth agave tones of this aged tequila come through when mixed with Grand Marnier (see previous recipe), so too do they blend wonderfully well with Cointreau.

> 1 lemon or lime wedge
> Saucer of kosher salt (about ¼-inch deep)
> 1¼ ounces Centinela 100-percent blue agave añejo
>   tequila
> 1 ounce Cointreau
> 1½ ounces freshly squeezed lemon or lime juice
> Ice

Run the lemon or lime wedge around the rim of a hurricane-style margarita glass. Dip the rim of the glass into the saucer of salt, rotating the rim in the salt until the desired amount has collected on the glass.

Measure the tequila, Cointreau, and lemon or lime juice into a 16-ounce cocktail shaker glass full of ice. Place a stainless steel cocktail shaker over the glass, tapping the top to create a seal. Shake vigorously for about 5 seconds and pour into the salt-rimmed glass.

Margarita Tip A great party idea is to organize a blind tasting of tequilas and/or margaritas for your friends. Pour drinks made with different tequilas (both silver and gold), and compare notes. Make sure that guests arriving by car have designated drivers—they can be put in charge of pouring the drinks, coding them so guests don't know ahead of time the brands they are trying, and announcing the results.

Tequila Tidbit The word mezcal is derived from the words metl and valli, which mean "stew" or "concoction" in the ancient Nahuatl (Aztec) language.

EL AMOR DE ORO MARGARITA

Makes 1 margarita

The name of this drink, one of the most elegant margaritas in the world, translates to "The Golden Love."

1 lemon or lime wedge
Saucer of kosher salt (about ¼-inch deep)
1¼ ounces Centinela Tres Años 100-percent blue agave muy añejo tequila
1 ounce Cointreau
1½ ounces freshly squeezed lemon or lime juice
Ice

Run the lemon or lime wedge around the rim of a hurricane-style margarita glass. Dip the rim of the glass into the saucer of salt, rotating the rim in the salt until the desired amount has collected on the glass.

Measure the tequila, Cointreau, and lemon or lime juice into a 16-ounce cocktail shaker glass full of ice. Place a stainless steel cocktail shaker over the glass, tapping the top to create a seal. Shake vigorously for about 5 seconds and pour into the salt-rimmed glass.

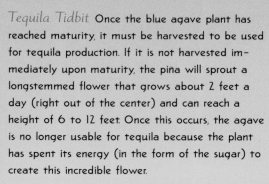

Margarita Tip An aged tequila can be savored in a snifter glass, as a fine cognac would, and sipped lovingly. Centinela Tres Años 100-percent blue agave tequila is aged for 3 years in oak barrels (by law, añejo tequila must be aged at least 1 year). This extra aging gives the liquor a rich golden hue and one of the deepest agave flavors of all tequilas on the market.

Tequila Tidbit Once the blue agave plant has reached maturity, it must be harvested to be used for tequila production. If it is not harvested immediately upon maturity, the piña will sprout a longstemmed flower that grows about 2 feet a day (right out of the center) and can reach a height of 6 to 12 feet. Once this occurs, the agave is no longer usable for tequila because the plant has spent its energy (in the form of the sugar) to create this incredible flower.

EL GRAN AGAVE DE ORO MARGARITA

Makes 1 margarita

In this margarita, we use Centinela Tres Años 100-percent agave muy añejo tequila. As its name implies, this tequila is put down to age on oak for at least 3 years, and the rewards are worth waiting for. The great thing about good superpremium agave tequila is that it generally has a good nose, and if you are a wine drinker, you know that the nose of the drink helps the enjoyment of the wine; well, this tequila has a great nose. The flavor is also exceptional—crisp, clean, and spicy, with no bitter aftertaste. Add Grand Marnier, and you will discover that this great añejo is one of the few that does not get overwhelmed by the cognac tones of the liqueur.

> 1 lemon or lime wedge
> Saucer of kosher salt (about ¼-inch deep)
> 1¼ ounces Centinela Tres Años 100-percent blue agave muy añejo tequila
> 1 ounce Grand Marnier
> 1½ ounces freshly squeezed lemon or lime juice
> Ice

Run the lemon or lime wedge around the rim of a hurricane-style margarita glass. Dip the rim of the glass into the saucer of salt, rotating the rim in the salt until the desired amount has collected on the glass.

Measure the tequila, Grand Marnier, and lemon or lime juice into a 16-ounce cocktail shaker glass full of ice. Place a stainless steel cocktail shaker over the glass, tapping the top to create a seal. Shake vigorously for about 5 seconds and pour into the salt-rimmed glass.

Tequila Tidbit The Aztecs used the agave plant as a food by roasting it over the fire and then eating the sweet flesh. They used the sap as a medicinal remedy, especially to heal wounds—like aloe vera. They also made the undistilled fermented juice into pulque, an alcoholic beverage.

Cabrito

Cabrito is the second label of Centinela and is located in Arandas (Los Altos), Jalisco. Centinela is one of the first superpremium tequilas that Maria's added to its list, the main reason being that Centinela is imported by a Santa Fe, New Mexico, importer, El Dorado Imports. Cabrito, on the other hand, is imported by Marsalle Co. in Cleveland. Cabrito 100-percent agave blanco, reposado, and gold come in a plain vanilla bottle—only the labels are different. Because it is a second label to Centinela, Cabrito is quite modestly priced—so much so, that we were able to offer a 100-percent agave margarita for less than five bucks (see the recipe for Maria's 100-percent Agave House Margarita on page 87). Cabrito is not as exquisite as its big brother, Centinela, but for the price it is one great tequila.

MARIA'S 100-PERCENT AGAVE HOUSE MARGARITA

Makes 1 margarita

Once you've discovered the magic of 100-percent agave tequilas, it's really tough to go back to one that's not a super-premium tequila, that is, less than 100-percent agave. In the first edition of this book, Maria's Real Margarita Book, *we suggested that only the likes of Michael Jordan or Michael Jackson could afford 100-percent agave tequila on an everyday basis, but Cabrito makes it possible for most of us after all! The price of Cabrito rivals the popular name labels that we have been buying for the last 50 years. In this recipe, we have mixed this great value with another one: Bols triple sec.*

> 1 lemon or lime wedge
> Saucer of kosher salt (about ¼-inch deep)
> 1¼ ounces Cabrito 100-percent agave blanco tequila
> 1 ounce Bols triple sec
> 1½ ounces freshly squeezed lemon or lime juice
> Ice

Run the lemon or lime wedge around the rim of a hurricane-style margarita glass. Dip the rim of the glass into the saucer of salt, rotating the rim in the salt until the desired amount has collected on the glass.

Measure the tequila, triple sec, and lemon or lime juice into a 16-ounce cocktail shaker glass full of ice. Place a stainless steel cocktail shaker over the glass, tapping the top to create a seal. Shake vigorously for about 5 seconds and pour into the salt-rimmed glass.

Margarita Tip You can, if you want, garnish your margarita with a lemon or lime slice, but you really don't need to. In any case, don't use any other garnish as it will impart its taste to the masterpiece you have just created.

Tequila Tidbit Try this tequila. It's not only affordable, but when it's used to make this margarita you'll love the way the nose of the agave wafts through the ice, and the way the taste of the natural sugars of agave, orange, and lemon hit the palate.

EL CABRITO DE PLATA MARGARITA
Makes 1 margarita

The expert mixologists at Maria's are of the opinion that any 100-percent agave tequila, regardless of cost, can and should be mixed with Cointreau or Grand Marnier. This is the same margarita as the previous one—Maria's "100-percent Agave House Margarita"—only instead of using the lower-cost triple sec, we use Cointreau. If you would like to have a really interesting and fun margarita tasting, compare margaritas made with Cabrito and triple sec to margaritas made with Cabrito and Cointreau.

> 1 lemon or lime wedge
> Saucer of kosher salt (about ¼-inch deep)
> 1¼ ounces Cabrito 100-percent agave blanco tequila
> 1 ounce Cointreau
> 1½ ounces freshly squeezed lemon or lime juice
> Ice

Run the lemon or lime wedge around the rim of a hurricane-style margarita glass. Dip the rim of the glass into the saucer of salt, rotating the rim in the salt until the desired amount has collected on the glass.

Measure the tequila, Cointreau, and lemon or lime juice into a 16-ounce cocktail shaker glass full of ice. Place a stainless steel cocktail shaker over the glass, tapping the top to create a seal. Shake vigorously for about 5 seconds and pour into the salt-rimmed glass.

Tequila Tidbit There is a wide variety in technique and technology when it comes to producing tequila. The larger producers, such as Cuervo and Sauza, use state-of-the-art technology, but the small "artisan" tequilas are handcrafted.

EL CABRITO DE ORO MARGARITA

Makes 1 margarita

Remember the tequila rules. If a tequila is 100-percent agave, it must be bottled at its source and exported in bottles only. Furthermore, for a tequila to be called "añejo," it must be aged on oak for at least 1 year while under the scrutiny of Mexican government inspectors. Cabrito 100-percent agave gold tequila does not claim to be añejo, so chances are the golden-colored tequila is artificially colored in the same manner as some of the popular brand gold tequilas—with caramel food coloring. Nonetheless, this is an excellent tequila and, at its modest price, a fantastic value.

> 1 lemon or lime wedge
> Saucer of kosher salt (about ¼-inch deep)
> 1¼ ounces Cabrito 100-percent agave gold tequila
> 1 ounce Cointreau
> 1½ ounces freshly squeezed lemon or lime juice
> Ice

Run the lemon or lime wedge around the rim of a hurricane-style margarita glass. Dip the rim of the glass into the saucer of salt, rotating the rim in the salt until the desired amount has collected on the glass.

Measure the tequila, Cointreau, and lemon or lime juice into a 16-ounce cocktail shaker glass full of ice. Place a stainless steel cocktail shaker over the glass, tapping the top to create a seal. Shake vigorously for about 5 seconds and pour into the salt-rimmed glass.

Margarita Tip Because of the alcohol content of margaritas (see tip on page 46), we recommend eating something hearty to minimize the absorption into the bloodstream. If you drink more than a couple over a short period of time, please don't drive.

Tequila Tidbit Aficionados will tell you that agave maturity will strongly influence tequila quality. Some big producers who rely on mass production tend to rely on less perfectly mature agaves than the small producers whose output is much smaller in scale.

THE GRAND LORENZO MARGARITA
Makes 1 margarita

Larry Felton, Maria's lead bartender, has probably mixed and hand-shaken more real margaritas than any one person in the world. Larry usually mixes 1,500 to 2,500 margaritas a week, and he's been doing it since 1990—he only missed a couple of weeks when he broke his collarbone. When he returned, he was shaking margaritas with his cast still on! By our estimates, he's closing in on his millionth margarita. So it goes without saying that if anyone in the world deserves a margarita dedicated and named for them, it's Maria's own Lawrence—"Don Lorenzo." Besides, he's a grand guy, so we mixed the Cabrito 100-percent agave reposado tequila with Grand Marnier to create a cocktail he can be proud of.

> 1 lemon or lime wedge
> Saucer of kosher salt (about ¼-inch deep)
> 1¼ ounces Cabrito 100-percent agave reposado tequila
> 1 ounce Grand Marnier
> 1½ ounces freshly squeezed lemon or lime juice
> Ice

Run the lemon or lime wedge around the rim of a hurricane-style margarita glass. Dip the rim of the glass into the saucer of salt, rotating the rim in the salt until the desired amount has collected on the glass.

Measure the tequila, Grand Marnier, and lemon or lime juice into a 16-ounce cocktail shaker glass full of ice. Place a stainless steel cocktail shaker over the glass, tapping the top to create a seal. Shake vigorously for about 5 seconds and pour into the salt-rimmed glass.

Tequila Tidbit Although by the Mexican government's legal definition, tequila can be made in any one of five states, over 95 percent of all tequila is distilled in the state of Jalisco.

Lapiz Azul

If you have spotted an unusual, dark blue handblown glass pyramid bottle in the tequila section of your favorite bar's back shelf, then this is it. When we were originally introduced to this tequila, my first thought was, "Just another pretty bottle"—but not so! Lo and behold, the stuff inside that blue pyramid was one of the most smooth and mellow 100-percent agave añejo tequilas that I've ever tasted. Named for the blue lapis semiprecious stone, this nectar of the gods is not blue itself, but rather a light flaxen color, reflecting the months spent on oak. You're going to pay a little extra for this great tequila because of the hard-to-produce bottle—but then again, you're going to love the bottle; it's one of the most requested "empties" we have at Maria's.

THE LAPIZ AZUL MARGARITA
Makes 1 margarita

To be perfectly honest, when I first saw the unusual bottle in which they ship Lapiz tequila to the United States, I smelled an impressive marketing gimmick. But when I mixed a Maria's margarita using Lapiz and Cointreau, I was shocked to taste one of the smoothest, most mellow margaritas (with just the proper amount of sweetness) that I have ever tasted. I was so excited by the flavor and smoothness of this margarita that I had to share it immediately with our customers. Well, they have voted with their tastebuds, and many have now made it their regular margarita. Give this recipe a try; not only will you love the bottle and never throw it away, you'll also love the margarita!

> 1 lemon or lime wedge
> Saucer of kosher salt (about ¼-inch deep)
> 1¼ ounces Tequila Lapiz 100-percent agave añejo
>   tequila
> 1 ounce Cointreau
> 1½ ounces freshly squeezed lemon or lime juice
> Ice

Run the lemon or lime wedge around the rim of a hurricane-style margarita glass. Dip the rim of the glass into the saucer of salt, rotating the rim in the salt until the desired amount has collected on the glass.

Measure the tequila, Cointreau, and lemon or lime juice into a 16-ounce cocktail shaker glass full of ice. Place a stainless steel cocktail shaker over the glass, tapping the top to create a seal. Shake vigorously for about 5 seconds and pour into the salt-rimmed glass.

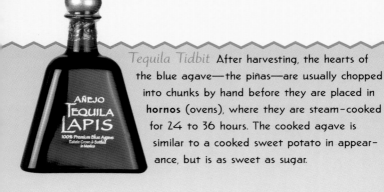

Tequila Tidbit After harvesting, the hearts of the blue agave—the piñas—are usually chopped into chunks by hand before they are placed in **hornos** (ovens), where they are steam-cooked for 24 to 36 hours. The cooked agave is similar to a cooked sweet potato in appearance, but is as sweet as sugar.

THE CROWN JEWELS MARGARITA
Makes 1 margarita

Lapis lazuli is a semiprecious stone that has a deep blue color—the Tequila Lapiz bottle emulates that color. When we were experimenting with this tequila to develop a suitable margarita, we shook it with Grand Marnier, freshly squeezed lemon juice, and ice. Then we poured it into a crystal hurricane margarita glass, ice and all, and it literally glistened like jewels. Given the Lapiz tequila, it seemed natural to call this drink "The Crown Jewels." When you mix this one up, you'll agree it's good, and you are unlikely to sit and admire the appearance for long!

>   1 lemon or lime wedge
>   Saucer of kosher salt (about ¼-inch deep)
>   1¼ ounces Tequila Lapiz 100-percent agave añejo
>   tequila
>   1 ounce Grand Marnier
>   1½ ounces freshly squeezed lemon or lime juice
>   Ice

Run the lemon or lime wedge around the rim of a hurricane-style margarita glass. Dip the rim of the glass into the saucer of salt, rotating the rim in the salt until the desired amount has collected on the glass.

Measure the tequila, Grand Marnier, and lemon or lime juice into a 16-ounce cocktail shaker glass full of ice. Place a stainless steel cocktail shaker over the glass, tapping the top to create a seal. Shake vigorously for about 5 seconds and pour into the salt-rimmed glass.

Tequila Tidbit After the agave hearts have been cooked, they are left to cool for up to 36 hours to maximize the amount of natural starches that are converted to sugar. The cooked agave is then crushed to remove the sweet juice (**aguamiel**) that will become tequila. It is left to ferment in tanks, usually with the help of added yeast.

THE PLATINUM PYRAMID
Makes 1 margarita

Generally, tequila importers begin their marketing in the United States with a silver or fresh-from-the-still product. Lapiz was first imported as añejo and did very well, gaining a reputation as a smooth sipping tequila, and in our Lapiz Azul and Crown Jewels margaritas. The unique bottle design, a blue pyramid, contributed to its acceptance in the American market. So much so, that the importer has now begun importing the silver Lapiz in the same pyramid bottle, but instead of the deep blue color, this one is a frosted silver glass. Add this silver to Cointreau and you've got The Platinum Pyramid.

> 1 lemon or lime wedge
> Saucer of kosher salt (about ¼-inch deep)
> 1¼ ounces Lapiz 100-percent agave silver tequila
> 1 ounce Cointreau
> 1½ ounces freshly squeezed lemon or lime juice
> Ice

Run the lemon or lime wedge around the rim of a hurricane-style margarita glass. Dip the rim of the glass into the saucer of salt, rotating the rim in the salt until the desired amount has collected on the glass.

Measure the tequila, Cointreau, and lemon or lime juice into a 16-ounce cocktail shaker glass full of ice. Place a stainless steel cocktail shaker over the glass, tapping the top to create a seal. Shake vigorously for about 5 seconds and pour into the salt-rimmed glass.

Tequila Tidbit **Don't be confused. There are three types (styles) of tequila. Some distillers use different names for these types. Tequila blanco is the same as "white" or "silver," and some are even calling it "platinum." Tequila reposado is sometimes called "gold" or even "aged" (truth is, it must be aged in oak, but only for as few as 90 days). Tequila añejo is sometimes called "gold," but most generally it is simply called "añejo" or aged; it must be aged on oak for at least a year.**

PLATINUM
TEQUILA
LAPIS
100% Premium Blue Agave
Estate Grown & Bottled
in Mexico

Gran Centenario

José Cuervo is the biggest producer of tequila in the world. It goes without saying that Cuervo will not just sit back and watch a bunch of boutique producers take over their share of the premium and superpremium tequila market. One of the ways they are doing this is to market Gran Centenario 100-percent agave plata, reposado, and añejo tequilas. Gran Centenario is imported by Carillon Importers Ltd., while most other Cuervo products are imported by Hueblein. The Gran Centenario plata is rested in new white oak casks, which results in a slight wooden tone in flavor and aroma, as well as in color, distinguishing it from all other silver tequilas. Their reposado is aged 6 months to 1 year in white oak casks, contributing to the brand's natural vanilla and clove tones. The añejo is aged 18 months in slightly charred white oak casks, which add to the mature, mellow full-bodied smoky complexity of this tequila. Even though these tequilas are handsomely packaged in beveled glass bottles with a distinctive label, reminiscent of the tequila's rich Mexican history, rest assured that you are paying for superpremium tequila and not flamboyant packaging.

THE DON BERNARDO MARGARITA
Makes 1 margarita

*Bernie Salazar has been associated with Maria's since 1987. He was
hired as a bartender, but he has worked his way up to management.
When we first added Gran Centenario 100-percent agave tequilas
(plata, reposado, and añejo) to our list, we discovered certain characteristics that Gran Centenario plata and Cointreau created together in
a margarita: Smooth. Mellow. Real. And whom do we associate with
these adjectives? Why, Bernie of course, but somehow, "Bernie's
Margarita" didn't flatter the margarita, so after much deliberation, we
came up with the slightly more formal "Don Bernardo." A fitting name
for this delicious margarita and a fitting tribute to Bernie, who has
become such an icon at Maria's.*

> 1 lemon or lime wedge
> Saucer of kosher salt (about ¼-inch deep)
> 1¼ ounces Gran Centenario 100-percent agave plata
>   tequila
> 1 ounce Cointreau
> 1½ ounces freshly squeezed lemon or lime juice
> Ice

Run the lemon or lime wedge around the rim of a hurricane-
style margarita glass. Dip the rim of the glass into the saucer
of salt, rotating the rim in the salt until the desired amount
has collected on the glass.

   Measure the tequila, Cointreau, and lemon or lime juice
into a 16-ounce cocktail shaker glass full of ice. Place a stainless steel cocktail shaker over the glass, tapping the top to
create a seal. Shake vigorously for about 5 seconds and pour
into the salt-rimmed glass.

Tequila Tidbit The blue agave reproduces in
two ways. The underground roots produce spider-
like offspring (see page 63 for the correct termi-
nology). In addition, to be on the safe side,
evolution has programmed the fully mature plant
to flower, set seed, and then die. The plants are
harvested for tequila before this dramatic conclusion is reached.

EL GRAN CENTENARIO MARGARITA
Makes 1 margarita

When the leading producer of tequila in the world decides to get into the superpremium 100-percent agave tequila game, it is already a couple of centuries ahead of the rest of the superpremium producers. That's why it was such a pleasure to see José Cuervo begin production of their Gran Centenario line. How can we put this? If Michael Jordan knows how to play basketball, José Cuervo knows how to make tequila. Cuervo is not making a big deal out of the fact that they are the makers of this tequila; they want it to succeed on its own merits. Try all three styles of Gran Centenario. This recipe calls for the reposado.

1 lemon or lime wedge
Saucer of kosher salt (about ¼-inch deep)
1¼ ounces Gran Centenario 100-percent agave reposado tequila
1 ounce Cointreau
1½ ounces freshly squeezed lemon or lime juice
Ice

Run the lemon or lime wedge around the rim of a hurricane-style margarita glass. Dip the rim of the glass into the saucer of salt, rotating the rim in the salt until the desired amount has collected on the glass.

Measure the tequila, Cointreau, and lemon or lime juice into a 16-ounce cocktail shaker glass full of ice. Place a stainless steel cocktail shaker over the glass, tapping the top to create a seal. Shake vigorously for about 5 seconds and pour into the salt-rimmed glass.

Margarita Tip If fresh lemons or limes are not available for squeezing, we suggest you use the commercially bottled Realemon, which is available in most grocery stores. Realemon is pure lemon juice with a small amount of preservative added; however, once opened, its shelf life is limited—2 or 3 days in the refrigerator at most—so be prepared to use it up or throw the rest away.

Tequila Tidbit In 1995, the Mexican government planned to raise the minimum amount of agave in tequila from 51 percent to 60 percent. However, for a number of reasons, these plans were never implemented.

EL GRAN CENTENARIO AÑEJO MARGARITA
Makes 1 margarita

José Cuervo produces more tequila than any distillery in Mexico (which also means the most in the world). When they produce a 100-percent agave añejo tequila—Gran Centenario—most tequila aficionados sit up and take notice. May we suggest, for a fun evening of tasting and experimenting with tequila and margaritas, that you buy a bottle of each of the Gran Centenario tequilas (plata, reposado, and añejo), a bottle of Cointreau, and a few dozen lemons or limes (for your freshly squeezed juice), and conduct a taste test of all three (see the previous pages for plata and reposado recipes).

1 lemon or lime wedge
Saucer of kosher salt (about ¼-inch deep)
1¼ ounces Gran Centenario 100-percent agave añejo tequila
1 ounce Cointreau
1½ ounces freshly squeezed lemon or lime juice
Ice

Run the lemon or lime wedge around the rim of a hurricane-style margarita glass. Dip the rim of the glass into the saucer of salt, rotating the rim in the salt until the desired amount has collected on the glass.

Measure the tequila, Cointreau, and lemon or lime juice into a 16-ounce cocktail shaker glass full of ice. Place a stainless steel cocktail shaker over the glass, tapping the top to create a seal. Shake vigorously for about 5 seconds and pour into the salt-rimmed glass.

Tequila Tidbit The maximum period for aging tequila in wooden barrels is 3 to 4 years. It is one spirit that does not improve with longer aging. After 6 or 7 years in the barrel, tequila becomes unpalatable.

1921

1921 is new on the scene, having been in existence only since the mid-1990s. It is produced by Agave Tequilana Productores y Comercialzadores in the small village of Jesus Maria. They produce 1921 in silver, reposado, and añejo. This tequila is imported by Water Street Imports, Ltd., in Houston, Texas. Similar to El Tesoro, 1921 is made the old-fashioned way—using a huge stone grinding wheel to crush the cooked agave. Like El Tesoro, the agave fibers are left in the fermentation tanks; consequently, you get a huge agave nose from each of the styles of 1921. By the way, the producers of 1921 and the producers of El Tesoro are cousins. Oh, there's more! Each bottle is unique and another "saver"! The 1921 is packaged in a handblown glass bottle with a pottery label embedded in the bottle—it's very attractive and the manufacturer goes so far as to seal the cork in wax, with a rawhide strip in the wax to facilitate opening.

THE 1921 SILVER DOLLAR MARGARITA

Makes 1 margarita

Silver dollars were as much a part of the settling of the West as saddles and chaps. When I was a youngster growing up in Santa Fe, I had a collection of the 100-percent silver dollars. My two oldest ones were dated 1881 and 1921. So when our margarita committee started experimenting with the 1921 100-percent agave plata tequila, I just had to name it "The 1921 Silver Dollar" (remember, plata means "silver"). So this is one margarita that had a name before it was even invented. What a great tequila! What a great bottle! What a great margarita! Sip this cocktail and let your mind drift back to 1921 when some rough and tumble cowboy in Santa Fe was spending that 1921 silver dollar at his favorite bar for a bottle of tequila.

    1 lemon or lime wedge
    Saucer of kosher salt (about ¼-inch deep)
    1¼ ounces 1921 100-percent agave plata tequila
    1 ounce Cointreau
    1½ ounces freshly squeezed lemon or lime juice
    Ice

Run the lemon or lime wedge around the rim of a hurricane-style margarita glass. Dip the rim of the glass into the saucer of salt, rotating the rim in the salt until the desired amount has collected on the glass.

Measure the tequila, Cointreau, and lemon or lime juice into a 16-ounce cocktail shaker glass full of ice. Place a stainless steel cocktail shaker over the glass, tapping the top to create a seal. Shake vigorously for about 5 seconds and pour into the salt-rimmed glass.

Tequila Tidbit Essential Spanish for the self-respecting tequilista:

Jimador or mescalero—the agave field workers;

Piña—the heart of the agave plant used to make tequila;

Coa—the tool used to harvest the piñas.

THE SMOOTH SIOUX MARGARITA
Makes 1 margarita

Let's clear up any misconception that this margarita has anything to do with the Sioux Nation. One of Maria's long-time servers spells her name "Sioux"—and this margarita is named after her. Sioux is one of those special people with a "hard as nails" disposition and a heart of gold. When we first experimented with the 1921 100-percent agave reposado tequila, we made up margaritas according to our regular formula—one with Cointreau and one with Grand Marnier. The one made with Cointreau was so smooth, yet a bit spicy, while the one made with Grand Marnier was a bit too strong for this delicate reposado. As we tasted the Cointreau with the 1921 reposado, a wonderful concoction, our first thought was "smooth"—then someone said, "smooth Sue." What better margarita to salute our own "Smooth Sioux"!

> 1 lemon or lime wedge
> Saucer of kosher salt (about ¼-inch deep)
> 1¼ ounces 1921 100-percent agave reposado tequila
> 1 ounce Cointreau
> 1½ ounces freshly squeezed lemon or lime juice
> Ice

Run the lemon or lime wedge around the rim of a hurricane-style margarita glass. Dip the rim of the glass into the saucer of salt, rotating the rim in the salt until the desired amount has collected on the glass.

Measure the tequila, Cointreau, and lemon or lime juice into a 16-ounce cocktail shaker glass full of ice. Place a stainless steel cocktail shaker over the glass, tapping the top to create a seal. Shake vigorously for about 5 seconds and pour into the salt-rimmed glass.

Tequila Tidbit All tequilas are double-distilled. In the case of 100-percent agave tequila, that means simply that the fermented agave juices (**aguamiel**, literally "honey water") are distilled once, then distilled a second time into a ready-to-drink, clear, fresh product that can be bottled as a white or silver tequila immediately, or held in stainless steel tanks until the distiller is ready to bottle.

THE 1921 GOLD COIN MARGARITA
Makes 1 margarita

This margarita is made with 1921 100-percent agave single-barrel añejo tequila, and you will love the attractively packaged handblown bottle. But the fun doesn't stop there. Once you break the waxed seal by pulling the rawhide strip and then remove the cork, you'll know that the 1921 tequila folks have managed to capture the grand essence of the agave. The deep golden color of this añejo reflects the extra care taken in leaving it on oak. Try it mixed as a margarita with dinner, then serve it, neat, in brandy snifters after dinner.

> 1 lemon or lime wedge
> Saucer of kosher salt (about ¼-inch deep)
> 1¼ ounces 1921 100-percent agave añejo tequila
> 1 ounce Cointreau
> 1½ ounces freshly squeezed lemon or lime juice
> Ice

Run the lemon or lime wedge around the rim of a hurricane-style margarita glass. Dip the rim of the glass into the saucer of salt, rotating the rim in the salt until the desired amount has collected on the glass.

Measure the tequila, Cointreau, and lemon or lime juice into a 16-ounce cocktail shaker glass full of ice. Place a stainless steel cocktail shaker over the glass, tapping the top to create a seal. Shake vigorously for about 5 seconds and pour into the salt-rimmed glass.

Tequila Tidbit Some distillers will manufacture tequila for more than one importer. The one producer can sell his tequila to as many "brands" as he likes or as many as the traffic will bear. However, the producer's NOM numbers will remain the same on all the brands he produces. Thus all of Cuervo's brands have the same NOM number; likewise for Sauza and Herradura, for example.

Casta

What happens when you own a glass factory and you decide to start marketing 100-percent agave tequila? You use a different designer bottle for every tequila you produce. That's exactly the case with Casta tequila. The flagship of the line is the Casta añejo, which is bottled in a handblown glass square with a huge neck and a cork and wood stopper. In the inside bottom of the bottle is a beautiful glass sculpture of an agave plant. The crowning achievement of this tequila producer is its Gusano brand, which is packaged in a bottle in the shape of a worm! The entire line is 100-percent agave and made at the Tequilera Newton e Hijos in Jalisco.

LA CASTA DE ORO MARGARITA
Makes 1 margarita

The Casta Oro reposado tequila is made with a different twist: it is 100-percent agave tequila that has been aged on oak for several months, then has some tequila añejo added, contributing "strength and vitality to its nature" (or so the label tells us). You will love the decanter-style hand-blown glass bottle that this tequila comes in. Casta Oro is labeled a reposado tequila, but Casta also produces a reposado called "Casta Brava" (see page 105) and a reposado called "Gusano" (see page 108). The addition of the añejo gives this tequila reposado a unique flavor that makes it stand out; when you make this margarita, you'll notice a stronger tequila taste that comes through the Cointreau and lemon juice.

> 1 lemon or lime wedge
> Saucer of kosher salt (about ¼-inch deep)
> 1¼ ounces Casta Oro 100-percent agave reposado
>   tequila
> 1 ounce Cointreau
> 1½ ounces freshly squeezed lemon or lime juice
> Ice

Run the lemon or lime wedge around the rim of a hurricane-style margarita glass. Dip the rim of the glass into the saucer of salt, rotating the rim in the salt until the desired amount has collected on the glass.

Measure the tequila, Cointreau, and lemon or lime juice into a 16-ounce cocktail shaker glass full of ice. Place a stainless steel cocktail shaker over the glass, tapping the top to create a seal. Shake vigorously for about 5 seconds and pour into the salt-rimmed glass.

Margarita Tip People tend to serve margaritas only with Mexican food. Next time you invest in a superpremium bottle of tequila, don't let it sit on a shelf until your next fiesta. Try serving about 1½ ounces of 100-percent blue agave tequila in brandy snifters after dinner instead of cognac. Your guests will marvel at your good taste and sophistication.

Tequila Tidbit While there are 360 varieties of agave, blue agave is the only one from which tequila can be made. Some of the other varieties are used to make mezcal and pulque, for example.

LA CASTA BRAVA MARGARITA
Makes 1 margarita

The Casta line of 100-percent agave tequilas ranges from moderately priced to expensive. Their Casta Brava 100-percent agave reposado tequila is at the moderate end of the scale, and it comes in an attractive, tall, pyramid-shaped handblown glass bottle. Open the bottle by removing the handsome wooden stopper, and enjoy the tequila's agave nose. Now taste a little in a snifter glass and you'll agree . . . strong . . . but not too strong. As a matter of fact, the word "brava" in Spanish means "brave" or "strong."

- 1 lemon or lime wedge
- Saucer of kosher salt (about ¼-inch deep)
- 1¼ ounces Casta Brava 100-percent agave reposado tequila
- 1 ounce Cointreau
- 1½ ounces freshly squeezed lemon or lime juice
- Ice

Run the lemon or lime wedge around the rim of a hurricane-style margarita glass. Dip the rim of the glass into the saucer of salt, rotating the rim in the salt until the desired amount has collected on the glass.

Measure the tequila, Cointreau, and lemon or lime juice into a 16-ounce cocktail shaker glass full of ice. Place a stainless steel cocktail shaker over the glass, tapping the top to create a seal. Shake vigorously for about 5 seconds and pour into the salt-rimmed glass.

Tequila Tidbit As you drive to Tequila from the city of Guadalajara (Mexico's second largest city), you begin to understand why they named **Agave tequilana Weber** the "blue agave." On either side of the narrow, two-lane asphalt highway is acre after acre of neat rows of huge agave plants. In the breeze, these noble plants create an ocean of brilliant azure as the sun highlights the blue-green color of their swordlike leaves.

LA CASTA AÑEJO MARGARITA
Makes 1 margarita

This margarita is made with one of the great-tasting 100-percent agave añejo tequilas. This tequila comes in a bottle that all our customers want (when it's empty, of course—they know we're not going to give them a full bottle). It features a glass sculpted agave plant on the inside of the handblown bottle. The bottle alone is almost worth the price, but you get the added bonus of being able to enjoy a wonderful añejo tequila. We think it's most enjoyable in a margarita, but try a bit in a snifter as well as in this recipe.

> 1 lemon or lime wedge
> Saucer of kosher salt (about ¼-inch deep)
> 1¼ ounces Casta 100-percent agave añejo tequila
> 1 ounce Cointreau
> 1½ ounces freshly squeezed lemon or lime juice
> Ice

Run the lemon or lime wedge around the rim of a hurricane-style margarita glass. Dip the rim of the glass into the saucer of salt, rotating the rim in the salt until the desired amount has collected on the glass.

Measure the tequila, Cointreau, and lemon or lime juice into a 16-ounce cocktail shaker glass full of ice. Place a stainless steel cocktail shaker over the glass, tapping the top to create a seal. Shake vigorously for about 5 seconds and pour into the salt-rimmed glass.

Margarita Tip Different tequilas, as well as different combinations of triple sec, Cointreau, and Grand Marnier, are what make margaritas so flexible. The different possibilities make experimenting with margaritas so much fun.

Tequila Tidbit The word **agave** is a botanical term derived from the Greek for "noble"—which seems highly appropriate to us!

LA CASTA GRANDE MARGARITA
Makes 1 margarita

When a really great tequila comes along, we at Maria's try it in our standard margarita recipe using Cointreau in one version and Grand Marnier in another. Generally, we settle for one or the other to put on our margarita list, but we found the Casta añejo tequila was so good with both liqueurs that we decided to put both on our list. The word grande means "big," and the flavor of this margarita is all of that. There is a spicy sweetness that comes from the oak barrels used to age this tequila, and in this recipe, the Grand Marnier seems to accentuate it with delicious results. This is probably the most outstanding of the Casta margaritas.

    1 lemon or lime wedge
    Saucer of kosher salt (about ¼-inch deep)
    1¼ ounces Casta 100-percent agave añejo tequila
    1 ounce Grand Marnier
    1½ ounces freshly squeezed lemon or lime juice
    Ice

Run the lemon or lime wedge around the rim of a hurricane-style margarita glass. Dip the rim of the glass into the saucer of salt, rotating the rim in the salt until the desired amount has collected on the glass.

Measure the tequila, Grand Marnier, and lemon or lime juice into a 16-ounce cocktail shaker glass full of ice. Place a stainless steel cocktail shaker over the glass, tapping the top to create a seal. Shake vigorously for about 5 seconds and pour into the salt-rimmed glass.

Tequila Tidbit How do the agave growers know when it's time to harvest the plants for tequila production? Reddish-orange colored patches appear on the base of the leaves and the plant appears to shrink a little from its regular height as the leaf sap is drawn into the heart of the plant (the piña).

EL GUSANO MARGARITA

Makes 1 margarita

You're going to have more fun with the bottle on this one than you are with the margarita. Don't be confused—a bottle of real tequila will never have a worm inside, but in this case, a worm can have a real tequila inside! This bottle from the Casta family of tequilas is in the shape of the cutest worm you've seen in a long time. The stopper is the head of the worm, complete with eyes, nose, and antennae, and the body consists of the handblown glass bottle shaped horizontally, complete with feet. Perhaps the surprising thing is that this tequila is getting rave reviews from tequila aficionados—it's an excellent 100 percent agave reposado tequila. Because of the unusual bottle, you'll pay a bit extra for this reposado, but be warned! Your guests will want the bottle!

> 1 lemon or lime wedge
> Saucer of kosher salt (about ¼-inch deep)
> 1¼ ounces Gusano 100-percent agave reposado tequila
> 1 ounce Cointreau
> 1½ ounces freshly squeezed lemon or lime juice
> Ice

Run the lemon or lime wedge around the rim of a hurricane-style margarita glass. Dip the rim of the glass into the saucer of salt, rotating the rim in the salt until the desired amount has collected on the glass.

Measure the tequila, Cointreau, and lemon or lime juice into a 16-ounce cocktail shaker glass full of ice. Place a stainless steel cocktail shaker over the glass, tapping the top to create a seal. Shake vigorously for about 5 seconds and pour into the salt-rimmed glass.

Margarita Tip As in any culture, in Mexico there are all kinds of toasts to make when enjoying a drink with friends. Some toasts are simply translations from one language to another. The most common toast in the Spanish language is "Salud" (which, accompanied with the lifting of a margarita glass, means "to your health").

Tequila Tidbit Tequila bottles never, ever, contain a worm (actually a moth larva). Instead, the worm can be found in some brands of mezcal.

Jesus Reyes

Jesus Reyes Cortes is one of the smaller but more established distillers located in the village of Tequila. Two types of tequila from this distiller are available in the U.S. market: Tequila de Don Jesus Reserva Familiar 100-percent agave reposado—an excellent value for money—and Tequila Añejo d'Reyes Reserva Seleccionada 100-percent agave, which likewise reflects a hands-on quality that comes from many good small producers.

LA MARGARITA DE DON JESUS
Makes 1 margarita

The name of this margarita has no religious significance. Pronounce the word "Jesus" the Mexican way—"hay-soose"—and the word takes on a rather different connotation to an English-speaking audience, don't you think? Okay, with that out of the way, let's talk about the tequila that goes into this margarita. The 100-percent reposado tequila made by Jesus Reyes Cortes blends extremely well with Cointreau and creates a smooth margarita with a mellow spiciness and no bitter aftertaste.

    1 lemon or lime wedge
    Saucer of kosher salt (about ¼-inch deep)
    1¼ ounces Tequila de Don Jesus Reserva Familiar 100-
        percent agave reposado
    1 ounce Cointreau
    1½ ounces freshly squeezed lemon or lime juice
    Ice

Run the lemon or lime wedge around the rim of a hurricane-style margarita glass. Dip the rim of the glass into the saucer of salt, rotating the rim in the salt until the desired amount has collected on the glass.

Measure the tequila, Cointreau, and lemon or lime juice into a 16-ounce cocktail shaker glass full of ice. Place a stainless steel cocktail shaker over the glass, tapping the top to create a seal. Shake vigorously for about 5 seconds and pour into the salt-rimmed glass.

Tequila Tidbit Blue agave plants have very shallow roots—no more than 1 foot underground. The harvested plants average 40 to 80 pounds each; a few weigh as much as 200 pounds.

LA MARGARITA D'REYES RESERVA
Makes 1 margarita

*For this margarita, you'll need Tequila Añejo d'Reyes Reserva
Seleccionada 100-percent agave tequila. This outstanding añejo is
mixed with Cointreau to create an equally outstanding margarita. I
have always liked the products from smaller producers. It's quite like
the abundance of boutique wineries in Napa Valley that, more often
than not, produce awesome wines. This same reasoning applies to this
tequila and this special margarita. See if you don't agree.*

> 1 lemon or lime wedge
> Saucer of kosher salt (about ¼-inch deep)
> 1¼ ounces Tequila Añejo d'Reyes Reserva Seleccionada
>   100-percent agave
> 1 ounce Cointreau
> 1½ ounces freshly squeezed lemon or lime juice
> Ice

Run the lemon or lime wedge around the rim of a hurricane-
style margarita glass. Dip the rim of the glass into the saucer
of salt, rotating the rim in the salt until the desired amount
has collected on the glass.

Measure the tequila, Cointreau, and lemon or lime juice
into a 16-ounce cocktail shaker glass full of ice. Place a stainless steel cocktail shaker over the glass, tapping the top to
create a seal. Shake vigorously for about 5 seconds and pour
into the salt-rimmed glass.

Margarita Tip It's no wonder that margaritas are associated
with good times and wonderful memories—it's a tradition. A
passage from a book called **Tequila, lo Nuestro** (published by
Sauza) reads in translation: "In every drop of tequila, of
our tequila, there is a spirit of the hospitality of our land
and the promise of a fiesta. Of a fiesta that never ends.
The fiesta of the tequila." Well, since the key ingredient
in a margarita is tequila, it stands to reason that good
times can be expected from drinking them.

Tequila Tidbit To learn even more about tequila,
invest in Lucinda Hutson's definitive work, called
(appropriately enough) ¡Tequila!, published by Ten
Speed Press. You will especially enjoy Lucinda's
wonderfully creative and mouthwatering recipes
that use the noble spirit.

Don Julio

Don Julio is a recent addition to the U.S. tequila market, but it should be readily available in most metropolitan areas. Currently, this 100-percent agave tequila is available in blanco and añejo.

THE DON JULIO PLATA MARGARITA

Makes 1 margarita

Of all the tequilas that we now have on our list, the one that was requested most often but was missing until 1998 (when the distributor finally was able to bring it into the state of New Mexico) was Tequila Reserva de Don Julio. The requests were well warranted—Don Julio is a wonderful tequila and it makes a fantastic margarita. When we mixed the Don Julio blanco tequila with Cointreau, we were absolutely delighted with the results. The fresh aroma of the agave emerges from the drink, and once the cool liquid hits the palate, you know you've got as good a tequila as you've ever tasted.

> 1 lemon or lime wedge
> Saucer of kosher salt (about ¼-inch deep)
> 1¼ ounces Reserva de Don Julio 100-percent agave
>   blanco tequila
> 1 ounce Cointreau
> 1½ ounces freshly squeezed lemon or lime juice
> Ice

Run the lemon or lime wedge around the rim of a hurricane-style margarita glass. Dip the rim of the glass into the saucer of salt, rotating the rim in the salt until the desired amount has collected on the glass.

Measure the tequila, Cointreau, and lemon or lime juice into a 16-ounce cocktail shaker glass full of ice. Place a stainless steel cocktail shaker over the glass, tapping the top to create a seal. Shake vigorously for about 5 seconds and pour into the salt-rimmed glass.

Margarita Tip In Spanish, the word **margarita** means "daisy." If you know anyone called Margarita, you can call her Daisy just to show off your phenomenal knowledge, but forget about going into a bar and ordering a "Daisy." They will only think you're strange (and bartenders don't take well to strange folk), and you'll never get your margarita!

Tequila Tidbit The word "tequila" is taken from the ancient Nahuatl (Aztec) language; it means "volcano." The village of Tequila is indeed set in the volcanic Sierra Madre mountains.

THE DON JULIO DE ORO MARGARITA

Makes 1 margarita

It seemed like it took forever for Don Julio to be imported into the state of New Mexico. We were getting constant requests at Maria's for Don Julio from out-of-state folks, especially those from California. Our distributor kept telling us that it would be available in "the next few months." Well, finally, in early 1998, we got our first shipment of Don Julio, and the wait was definitely worth it. The Don Julio 100-percent agave añejo tequila has tones of pepper and oak that settle on the back of the mouth. This is one of the better margaritas you'll ever shake up and serve!

> 1 lemon or lime wedge
> Saucer of kosher salt (about ¼-inch deep)
> 1¼ ounces Reserva de Don Julio 100-percent agave añejo tequila
> 1 ounce Cointreau
> 1½ ounces freshly squeezed lemon or lime juice
> Ice

Run the lemon or lime wedge around the rim of a hurricane-style margarita glass. Dip the rim of the glass into the saucer of salt, rotating the rim in the salt until the desired amount has collected on the glass.

Measure the tequila, Cointreau, and lemon or lime juice into a 16-ounce cocktail shaker glass full of ice. Place a stainless steel cocktail shaker over the glass, tapping the top to create a seal. Shake vigorously for about 5 seconds and pour into the salt-rimmed glass.

Tequila Tidbit The Mexican government introduced strict rules regarding the production of tequila in the 1970s for the purpose of ensuring quality standards. These rules, enshrined in law, are called "La Norma," or the Norm, the law.

EL GRAN JULIO RESERVA MARGARITA

Makes 1 margarita

For Maria's to use Grand Marnier in a margarita, we have to make sure that the strength of the Grand Marnier does not overwhelm the flavor of the tequila, using the tried-and-true proportions in our recipes. (We could add more tequila, but it would irresponsibly increase the alcohol intake by our customers; our aim is not to get anyone drunk, but rather to serve enjoyable margaritas with our great New Mexican food.) When we tested Reserva de Don Julio 100-percent agave añejo with Grand Marnier, not only did it hold up to the challenge of the liqueur, but the oak and pepper tones of this wonderful añejo came through like a champ.

> 1 lemon or lime wedge
> Saucer of kosher salt (about ¼-inch deep)
> 1¼ ounces Reserva de Don Julio 100-percent agave
>   añejo tequila
> 1 ounce Grand Marnier
> 1½ ounces freshly squeezed lemon or lime juice
> Ice

Run the lemon or lime wedge around the rim of a hurricane-style margarita glass. Dip the rim of the glass into the saucer of salt, rotating the rim in the salt until the desired amount has collected on the glass.

Measure the tequila, Grand Marnier, and lemon or lime juice into a 16-ounce cocktail shaker glass full of ice. Place a stainless steel cocktail shaker over the glass, tapping the top to create a seal. Shake vigorously for about 5 seconds and pour into the salt-rimmed glass.

Margarita Tip It can be fun to experiment with tequilas and other fruit-based liquors or juices—for example, a Melon Margarita made with tequila, Midori, and lemon juice; a Watermelon Margarita using watermelon juice instead of lemon juice; an Apple Margarita made with apple juice. Use cranberry juice, mango nectar— there's no limit. See the next chapter for some recipes.

Tequila Tidbit About 2,000 blue agave plants are grown per acre in tequila country, in neat, symmetrical rows.

Other Tequilas and Margaritas

As we enter into a new millennium, Maria's maintains a tequila list of about 100 real tequilas. We offer over 100 real margaritas. All of our tequilas are "real" tequilas—only a half dozen are not 100-percent agave.

Are you ready for this? As we enter the 21st century, Mexico is producing tequila (not all of which is 100-percent agave) under 348 different labels. Most of these tequilas are not being imported into the United States at the present time, and a lot of them are in very limited production.

Recently, in an attempt to improve the quality of all less-than-100-percent agave tequilas, the Mexican government tried to pass the requirement that all tequila be at least 60-percent agave to be considered a tequila. This attempt failed, as it was pointed out that the agave is in short supply; and since it takes so long for it to mature, it would be foolish to change something so well established and that would only create more supply problems. Remember: there are only five states in Mexico in which the agave used for tequila can be grown—watch for this to change after the turn of the century; other growing areas are bound to be added to the list because of the demand for tequila. On the other hand, however, it is said that there are so many new 100-percent agave tequilas being produced because the agave sugars are less expensive than cane sugar.

Here are recipes for margaritas made with some of those new brands that have recently found their way into the American market.

LA MARGARITA DE LOS DOS ANGELES

Makes 1 margarita

This margarita is named after two guys named Engles (Engles is German for "angels"). Los Dos Angeles means "The Two Angels," but neither of these guys are! They are friends of Maria's, and we just had to name a margarita after them. This margarita uses El Jimador 100-percent agave silver tequila, a moderately priced tequila and a quite good value. We mix it with Cointreau and freshly squeezed lemon juice to create the "Two Angels Margarita." Mix one up and see if you don't agree that, despite its name, this Margarita is a bit on the devilish side.

> 1 lemon or lime wedge
> Saucer of kosher salt (about ¼-inch deep)
> 1¼ ounces El Jimador 100-percent agave silver tequila
> 1 ounce Cointreau
> 1½ ounces freshly squeezed lemon or lime juice
> Ice

Run the lemon or lime wedge around the rim of a hurricane-style margarita glass. Dip the rim of the glass into the saucer of salt, rotating the rim in the salt until the desired amount has collected on the glass.

Measure the tequila, Cointreau, and lemon or lime juice into a 16-ounce cocktail shaker glass full of ice. Place a stainless steel cocktail shaker over the glass, tapping the top to create a seal. Shake vigorously for about 5 seconds and pour into the salt-rimmed glass.

Tequila Tidbit We are sometimes asked if the rumor that tequila is an aphrodisiac is true. Well, we like to think it is, but alas, there is no scientific evidence (yet) to support our wishful thinking.

THE MARGARITA EL JIMADOR
Makes 1 margarita

*El Jimador is wonderful 100-percent agave tequila that comes in a stan-
dard liquor bottle rather than a handblown object d'art, so you pay for
the juice, not the decanter. We use the El Jimador 100-percent agave
reposado tequila for this margarita, combining it with Cointreau and
our ever-present freshly squeezed lemon juice. The reposado has a deep
golden hue naturally acquired from its rest in oak barrels for at least 90
days. The flavor is full of agave with a mellow spicy finish, so it combines with the oranges in the Cointreau and the pure lemon juice to
make a very respectable margarita at a reasonable price.*

1 lemon or lime wedge
Saucer of kosher salt (about ¼-inch deep)
1¼ ounces El Jimador 100-percent agave reposado
   tequila
1 ounce Cointreau
1½ ounces freshly squeezed lemon or lime juice
Ice

Run the lemon or lime wedge around the rim of a hurricane-
style glass. Dip the rim of the glass into the saucer of salt,
rotating the rim in the salt until the desired amount has collected on the glass.

Measure the tequila, Cointreau, and lemon or lime juice
into a 16-ounce cocktail shaker glass full of ice. Place a stainless steel cocktail shaker over the glass, tapping the top to
create a seal. Shake vigorously for about 5 seconds and pour
into the salt-rimmed glass.

Tequila Tidbit By law, all tequila must be distilled
twice. The product of the first distillation is referred to
as *ordinario*. The second distillation brings the tequila to
its final proof, which, if over 80, must be diluted
down with water.

Margarita Tip If you plan to store any leftover
margaritas, whether it's a half a glass or a half
a punch bowl, be sure you remove any ice still
unmelted. Otherwise, the margarita will be very
watery the next day. A good margarita should
keep for a couple of days under refrigeration.

MARGARITA EL CABO WABO KEVIN

Makes 1 margarita

This tequila is a 100-percent agave reposado from Sammy Hagar's Club Cabo Wabo in the Baja. Sammy claims this tequila was a favorite of the Rolling Stones. We have used our own recipe to make a margarita that is a little bit crazy. That's why we call it the Cabo Wabo Kevin. You see, Kevin is a longtime waiter at Maria's in Santa Fe, and he is a little on the wabo-wabo side, if you get my drift. Kevin is an entertainer. He is the only person I know that can carry margaritas "two up" on the upturned palm of his hand without spilling. Kevin is a great guy, and his margarita is a great cocktail.

> 1 lemon or lime wedge
> Saucer of kosher salt (about ¼-inch deep)
> 1¼ ounces Cabo Wabo Terra-Firme 100-percent
>   reposado tequila
> 1 ounce Cointreau
> 1½ ounces freshly squeezed lemon or lime juice
> Ice

Run the lemon or lime wedge around the rim of a hurricane-style margarita glass. Dip the rim of the glass into the saucer of salt, rotating the rim in the salt until the desired amount has collected on the glass.

Measure the tequila, Cointreau, and lemon or lime juice into a 16-ounce cocktail shaker glass full of ice. Place a stainless steel cocktail shaker over the glass, tapping the top to create a seal. Shake vigorously for about 5 seconds and pour into the salt-rimmed glass.

Tequila Tidbit The average American household spent $227 on alcohol in 1997. A portion of that amount was for tequila. Tequila consumption has been growing at the rate of over 6 percent a year for the past few years. That increase is expected to grow even higher as more and more Americans become familiar with premium tequilas.

Margarita Tip Rocker Sammy Hagar serves the Cabo Waborita at his nightclub in Cabo San Lucas. This is the recipe: In a shaker over crushed ice, squeeze two fresh limes. Double that with Cointreau. Double that with Cabo Wabo tequila. Add a splash of Grand Marnier. For color, add a splash of blue curaçao. Shake and pour straight up into frozen salt-rimmed glasses. Makes two Cabo Waboritas.

THE DANDY RANDY RANDY
Makes 1 margarita

This margarita features a tequila that comes in the tallest spirits bottle that I have ever seen, and the flavor is even taller. The Dandy Randy Randy uses Corralejo 100-percent agave añejo tequila and Cointreau. It's named for an old friend and one of our best longtime employees, both of whom are named Randy and both of whom are dandies! We just couldn't call it a Randy margarita, because the two Randys would not know which Randy it was named after . . . this way, we have assured both Randys that it is indeed named after each one of them.

> 1 lemon or lime wedge
> Saucer of kosher salt (about ¼-inch deep)
> 1¼ ounces Corralejo 100-percent agave añejo tequila
> 1 ounce Cointreau
> 1½ ounces freshly squeezed lemon or lime juice
> Ice

Run the lemon or lime wedge around the rim of a hurricane-style margarita glass. Dip the rim of the glass into the saucer of salt, rotating the rim in the salt until the desired amount has collected on the glass.

Measure the tequila, Cointreau, and lemon or lime juice into a 16-ounce cocktail shaker glass full of ice. Place a stainless steel cocktail shaker over the glass, tapping the top to create a seal. Shake vigorously for about 5 seconds and pour into the salt-rimmed glass.

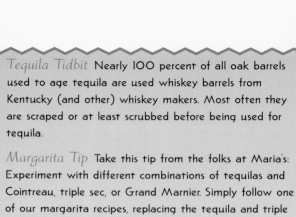

Tequila Tidbit Nearly 100 percent of all oak barrels used to age tequila are used whiskey barrels from Kentucky (and other) whiskey makers. Most often they are scraped or at least scrubbed before being used for tequila.

Margarita Tip Take this tip from the folks at Maria's: Experiment with different combinations of tequilas and Cointreau, triple sec, or Grand Marnier. Simply follow one of our margarita recipes, replacing the tequila and triple sec with your own ingredient. Once you've come up with the perfect combination, have friends over and name it after your best pal.

LA MARGARITA CAZADORES
Makes 1 margarita

I have been reading about Cazadores tequila for many years and was impressed by their distillery in Arandas, Jalisco. This tequila has only recently been imported into the United States and it is one of the best buys in a 100 percent agave reposado. Cazadores has been a favorite among the folks who live in Mexico for many years . . . most likely because it's a quality product and it is reasonably priced. For this margarita we have mixed Cazadores with Cointreau to come up with a mellow, dry, and great-tasting margarita.

> 1 lemon or lime wedge
> Saucer of kosher salt (about ¼-inch deep)
> 1¼ ounces Cazadores 100-percent reposado tequila
> 1 ounce Cointreau
> 1½ ounces freshly squeezed lemon or lime juice
> Ice

Run the lemon or lime wedge around the rim of a hurricane-style margarita glass. Dip the rim of the glass into the saucer of salt, rotating the rim in the salt until the desired amount has collected on the glass.

Measure the tequila, Cointreau, and lemon or lime juice into a 16-ounce cocktail shaker glass full of ice. Place a stainless steel cocktail shaker over the glass, tapping the top to create a seal. Shake vigorously for about 5 seconds and pour into the salt-rimmed glass.

Tequila Tidbit There are dozens of new tequilas entering the U.S. market annually. Most of the new tequilas are 100-percent agave and are brought in by new American importers trying to create a niche in the tequila market with clever names and/or packaging. Remember, it has to say, "bottled in Mexico" or "estate bottled at the Distillery" for it to be 100-percent agave.

Margarita Tip As long as you have tequila and Cointreau, triple sec, or Grand Marnier among your list of ingredients, it should be considered a margarita, regardless of the fruit or fruit juice you use in place of the lemon. If you use some other fruit, be sure it's ripe. You should generally blend it with ice.

THE JAILBIRD
Makes 1 margarita

I mean, what else can you name a margarita that is made with a tequila called Alcatraz? Alcatraz comes in one of the most beautiful bottles that we have ever seen, but the real beauty lies within. The tequila is 100-percent agave silver, and the freshness of this spirit is really brought out when we combine it with Cointreau and freshly squeezed lemon juice. The flavor of the agave comes through and is especially pronounced in its fresh silver nature unaltered by oak.

- 1 lemon or lime wedge
- Saucer of kosher salt (about ¼-inch deep)
- 1¼ ounces Alcatraz 100-percent agave silver tequila
- 1 ounce Cointreau
- 1½ ounces freshly squeezed lemon or lime juice
- Ice

Run the lemon or lime wedge around the rim of a hurricane-style margarita glass. Dip the rim of the glass into the saucer of salt, rotating the rim in the salt until the desired amount has collected on the glass.

Measure the tequila, Cointreau, and lemon or lime juice into a 16-ounce cocktail shaker glass full of ice. Place a stainless steel cocktail shaker over the glass, tapping the top to create a seal. Shake vigorously for about 5 seconds and pour into the salt rimmed glass.

Tequila Tidbit There is a new mezcal (tequila's illegitimate first cousin) on the market with a new twist. This mezcal, Sotol reposado, is made from the wild agave plant growing in the Chihuahuan Desert of northern Mexico. It comes from Hacienda de Chihuahua through Palm Bay Imports.

Margarita Tip Try to serve your margaritas in stemware. For its "rocks" glass, Maria's uses a hurricane-style glass made by Libbey, called the "Poco Grande." The "up" glass we use is also from Libbey and is called the "Coupette." If your favorite kitchen or bar supply store does not stock them, ask them to order by name from Libbey.

HUSSONG'S SPECIAL MARGARITA
Makes 1 margarita

According to the label, "Juan Hussong built the cantina (Hussong's in Ensenada, Mexico) in 1892 to accommodate fortune-seeking stagecoach riders. The cantina has since become a mecca for travelers from around the world who come to seek good times and good friends. In their search they discover still another treasure—a rare tequila that for many years was a well-hidden secret."

Hussong's used to describe itself as a 99-percent blue agave reposado tequila, but now the label reads "100 percent blue agave"—it is now bottled in Mexico. Formerly, in order to comply with Mexican government regulations, Hussong's could not claim to be 100 percent because it was shipped to the United States in bulk and bottled in Missouri.

At Hussong's cantina, the margaritas are made by mixing equal parts of Hussong's tequila, Cointreau, and lemon juice, and served over ice in a salt-rimmed glass.

> 1 lemon or lime wedge
> Saucer of kosher salt (about ¼-inch deep)
> 1¼ ounces Hussong's 100-percent agave tequila
> 1 ounce Cointreau
> 1½ ounces freshly squeezed lemon or lime juice
> Ice

Run the lemon or lime wedge around the rim of a hurricane-style margarita glass. Dip the rim of the glass into the saucer of salt, rotating the rim in the salt until the desired amount has collected on the glass.

Measure the tequila, Cointreau, and lemon or lime juice into a 16-ounce cocktail shaker glass full of ice. Place a stainless steel cocktail shaker over the glass, tapping the top to create a seal. Shake vigorously for about 5 seconds and pour into the salt-rimmed glass.

Tequila Tidbit The golden hue found in most aged tequilas (reposado, añejo, and muy añejo) comes from the oaken barrels in which the original white tequila is placed. The more aging the tequila has does not necessarily mean the darker gold it will be. The intensity of the color is dependent on both the duration of the aging process and the type of oak barrel that is used.

LA MARGARITA DE LAS TRANCAS
Makes 1 margarita

Given that Las Trancas was originally distilled by El Viejito, but more recently by Agroindustrias Guadalajara, you may want to seek out the latter, fresher tequila. If you have a bottle with the 1107 NOM, it was made at El Viejito, but if the bottle shows 1068 as the NOM number, it was made by Agroindustrias. The attractive handblown glass bottle, unlike most other tequilas packaged in unique bottles, does not seem to affect the price too much, which remains reasonable. Mix this outstanding tequila with Cointreau and you'll please anyone who tastes it.

    1 lemon or lime wedge
    Saucer of kosher salt (about ¼-inch deep)
    1¼ ounces Las Trancas 100-percent agave reposado
        tequila
    1 ounce Cointreau
    1½ ounces freshly squeezed lemon or lime juice
    Ice

Run the lemon or lime wedge around the rim of a hurricane-style margarita glass. Dip the rim of the glass into the saucer of salt, rotating the rim in the salt until the desired amount has collected on the glass.

Measure the tequila, Cointreau, and lemon or lime juice into a 16-ounce cocktail shaker glass full of ice. Place a stainless steel cocktail shaker over the glass, tapping the top to create a seal. Shake vigorously for about 5 seconds and pour into the salt-rimmed glass.

Margarita Tip Using commercial ice cubes in your margarita will give you two advantages: they are crystal clear and they are usually made from filtered water.

Tequila Tidbit The Tequila Producers Association (La Camera Regional de la Industria Tequilera) was formed in 1949 and has fewer than 30 members. Headquartered in Guadalajara, it is the trade group that promotes tequila throughout the world and helps maintain the highest standards of production.

THE RIO GRAND MARGARITA
Makes 1 margarita

The Rio Grande River dissects the state of New Mexico as it flows from southern Colorado through New Mexico and into Texas and eventually the Gulf of Mexico. Those of us who grew up around Santa Fe heard the Rio Grande referred to as the "Rio Grand." Now with all of the "grand" margaritas on our list, we searched and searched for an excuse to name one of our margaritas "The Rio Grand." We found a 100-percent agave añejo tequila that could not have been more perfect—Rio de Plata (River of Silver). Most of our margaritas that call for Grand Marnier use the word "Grand" in the name. This is no exception. Rio de Plata 100-percent agave añejo tequila, Grand Marnier, and freshly squeezed lemon juice could not be called anything other than "The Rio Grand"!

> 1 lemon or lime wedge
> Saucer of kosher salt (about ¼-inch deep)
> 1¼ ounces Rio de Plata 100-percent agave añejo tequila
> 1 ounce Grand Marnier
> 1½ ounces freshly squeezed lemon or lime juice
> Ice

Run the lemon or lime wedge around the rim of a hurricane-style margarita glass. Dip the rim of the glass into the saucer of salt, rotating the rim in the salt until the desired amount has collected on the glass.

Measure the tequila, Grand Marnier, and lemon or lime juice into a 16-ounce cocktail shaker glass full of ice. Place a stainless steel cocktail shaker over the glass, tapping the top to create a seal. Shake vigorously for about 5 seconds and pour into the salt-rimmed glass.

Tequila Tidbit Mezcal is made from other types of agave, which are roasted and distilled differently from tequila. The state of Oaxaca is one of the biggest producers; each village in the agricultural Oaxaca Valley boasts its own distinctive mezcal.

LA MARGARITA DEL DUEÑO
Makes 1 margarita

One thinks of a fine wine when referring to a beverage as "Reserva del Dueño" (Proprietor's Reserve). But when you taste this tequila, you understand what the distiller is trying to convey with the name; it's a prestigious description that applies equally well to this tequila. This is indeed the good stuff—the stuff that the owner or proprietor has held back for himself and his nearest and dearest! In this recipe, Reserva del Dueño is mixed with Cointreau and freshly squeezed lemon juice to make a margarita that could just as easily be called "The Proprietor's Reserve."

1 lemon or lime wedge
Saucer of kosher salt (about ¼-inch deep)
1¼ ounces Reserva del Dueño 100-percent agave añejo
    tequila
1 ounce Cointreau
1½ ounces freshly squeezed lemon or lime juice
Ice

Run the lemon or lime wedge around the rim of a hurricane-style margarita glass. Dip the rim of the glass into the saucer of salt, rotating the rim in the salt until the desired amount has collected on the glass.

Measure the tequila, Cointreau, and lemon or lime juice into a 16-ounce cocktail shaker glass full of ice. Place a stainless steel cocktail shaker over the glass, tapping the top to create a seal. Shake vigorously for about 5 seconds and pour into the salt-rimmed glass.

Margarita Tip Here's another toast offered in Mexico (imported from Spain); that's a little more elaborate than the simple "Salud": **Salud, dinero y amor; y tiempo para gustarlos.** ("Health, money, and love, and the time to enjoy them.")

Tequila Tidbit The amount and duration of heat during the fermentation process does affect the flavor and quality of the finished tequila. If the process takes a long time, and the mixture is not overheated, then it is more likely that the delicate flavors of the agave will show through.

LA MARGARITA DE LOS VALIENTES
Makes 1 margarita

When it comes to marketing and packaging, tequila makers take the cake. Los Valientes 100-percent agave reposado tequila comes in a plain old-fashioned bottle with a metal screw top, but it's dressed in a canvas sleeve shoulder-high on the bottle with a strip of rawhide laced through the brass eyelets. This tequila was created as a salute to the brave soldiers of the Mexican Revolution in Los Valientes, a squadron under the command of General Matias Ramos Santos, but those brave souls never heard of Cointreau—or of margaritas, for that matter. So when you mix this outstanding cocktail, raise your glass high and toast the squadron El Rayo—Los Valientes.

> 1 lemon or lime wedge
> Saucer of kosher salt (about ¼-inch deep)
> 1¼ ounces Los Valientes 100-percent agave reposado tequila
> 1 ounce Cointreau
> 1½ ounces freshly squeezed lemon or lime juice
> Ice

Run the lemon or lime wedge around the rim of a hurricane-style margarita glass. Dip the rim of the glass into the saucer of salt, rotating the rim in the salt until the desired amount has collected on the glass.

Measure the tequila, Cointreau, and lemon or lime juice into a 16-ounce cocktail shaker glass full of ice. Place a stainless steel cocktail shaker over the glass, tapping the top to create a seal. Shake vigorously for about 5 seconds and pour into the salt-rimmed glass.

Tequila Tidbit If you ever plan a trip to see the tequila distilleries, an indispensable guide is **The Tequila Lover's Guide to Mexico**, written by Lance Cutler and published by the Wine Patrol Press in 1998. Cutler, a California winemaker, taste-tests tequilas and offers a very helpful travel guide.

LA MARGARITA "VIVA MEXICO"
Makes 1 margarita

Every September 15th, a chorus of exuberant Mexicans gather outside the National Palace to raise their voices and repeat the 1810 cry for independence, "Viva Mexico." That cry is called "el grito" ("the yell"). Afterwards, in celebration, glasses are raised, filled with tequila. This margarita is a yell itself. As a matter of fact, we have some customers at Maria's who come up to the bar and shout, "Viva Mexico!" Our bartenders sometimes have to figure out if the customer is making a political statement or ordering a margarita. El Grito's clean and mellow finish makes this margarita one of the smoothest on our list. Pick it up if you see it on your dealer's shelf—you'll love the tequila and you'll shout the praises of this margarita!

    1 lemon or lime wedge
    Saucer of kosher salt (about ¼-inch deep)
    1¼ ounces El Grito 100-percent agave silver tequila
    1 ounce Cointreau
    1½ ounces freshly squeezed lemon or lime juice
    Ice

Run the lemon or lime wedge around the rim of a hurricane-style margarita glass. Dip the rim of the glass into the saucer of salt, rotating the rim in the salt until the desired amount has collected on the glass.

Measure the tequila, Cointreau, and lemon or lime juice into a 16-ounce cocktail shaker glass full of ice. Place a stainless steel cocktail shaker over the glass, tapping the top to create a seal. Shake vigorously for about 5 seconds and pour into the salt-rimmed glass.

Margarita Tip In addition to Realemon as a substitute for fresh lemon or lime juice, Minute Maid produces a frozen nonconcentrated pure lemon juice that has no additives. Under no circumstances should you use a sweetened lemon or lime juice such as frozen lemonade or frozen limeade. With the added sugar in these products, you'll end up with an icky-sweet margarita that's a waste of good tequila.

Tequila Tidbit Tequila does not share quite the long history of pulque or mezcal; it dates from the late seventeenth century, but production only began in earnest in the last quarter of the nineteenth century.

THE BOOGIE WOOGIE
Makes 1 margarita

The Boogie Woogie is made from a new entry in the 100-percent agave tequila imports, Chamuscos. Actually, Chamuscos means "Boogie Man" in Spanish, but margaritas are too much fun to introduce any kind of a negative as a name for one, so we went with the Boogie Woogie. After all there can't be much more fun than doing the boogie woogie—that is, until you've tried this margarita. Chamuscos is a 100-percent agave reposado tequila marketed in a tall bottle with a label that has all kinds of spirits and boogie men on it. Don't let the label scare you away . . . it's a great tequila.

> 1 lemon or lime wedge
> Saucer of kosher salt (about ¼-inch deep)
> 1¼ ounces Chamuscos 100-percent agave reposado
>   tequila
> 1 ounce Cointreau
> 1½ ounces freshly squeezed lemon or lime juice
> Ice

Run the lemon or lime wedge around the rim of a hurricane-style margarita glass. Dip the rim of the glass into the saucer of salt, rotating the rim in the salt until the desired amount has collected on the glass.

Measure the tequila, Cointreau, and lemon or lime juice into a 16-ounce cocktail shaker glass full of ice. Place a stainless steel cocktail shaker over the glass, tapping the top to create a seal. Shake vigorously for about 5 seconds and pour into the salt-rimmed glass.

Tequila Tidbit The blue agave used to make tequila is selected for its concentrated sugar content (A.R.T.). Industry standards are 20-percent minimum sugar concentrated agave. Most distillers try to exceed 25-percent A.R.T. agave. This allows for higher standards in quality and a more efficient fermentation and distillation.

Margarita Tip There is now a wide selection of colored salts specifically packaged for making margaritas. These should be available at your favorite bar or kitchen supply store. If you can't find them on your dealer's shelves, simply ask the proprietor to order them for you.

LA HACIENDA CORRALEJO MARGARITA

Makes 1 margarita

This margarita is made with Corralejo 100-percent agave reposado tequila. The bottle is handblown glass and stands nearly 2 feet tall. The label claims that the Hacienda Corralejo was established in 1755. I think this is the date of the hacienda, not the first production of tequila. Corralejo has the first label with a health warning in Spanish on it: "El abuso en el consumo de este producto es nocivo para la salud," which means, "The abuse in the consumption of this product is harmful to your health." This is great tequila, and in blind margarita tastings, it won the hearts of many of Maria's faithful. Mix it with Cointreau and enjoy.

> 1 lemon or lime wedge
> Saucer of kosher salt (about ¼-inch deep)
> 1¼ ounces Corralejo 100-percent agave reposado
>   tequila
> 1 ounce Cointreau
> 1½ ounces freshly squeezed lemon or lime juice
> Ice

Run the lemon or lime wedge around the rim of a hurricane-style margarita glass. Dip the rim of the glass into the saucer of salt, rotating the rim in the salt until the desired amount has collected on the glass.

Measure the tequila, Cointreau, and lemon or lime juice into a 16-ounce cocktail shaker glass full of ice. Place a stainless steel cocktail shaker over the glass, tapping the top to create a seal. Shake vigorously for about 5 seconds and pour into the salt-rimmed glass.

Tequila Tidbit The Zapotec and Mixtec Indians in the Oaxaca area would ferment the sap taken from the roots, stalks, and leaves of wild agave plants to create a drink now called **pulque**. Indians of Mexico still use pulque as a major home remedy. Medicinal herbs are often mixed with pulque to increase their benefit.

Margarita Tip Encourage your guests to enjoy their margaritas directly from the salt-rimmed glass, rather than through a straw. At Maria's we serve our margaritas with a straw, but it is only to be used as a stirrer. The salt creates a completely different taste.

EL CONQUISTADOR MARGARITA
Makes 1 margarita

Another new import into the United States is El Conquistador. El Conquistador comes in blanco, reposado, and añejo. This margarita is made with the 100-percent agave blanco tequila. El Conquistador is packaged in a very attractive handblown blue bottle with white and gold lettering. The blanco is reasonably priced and should be available throughout the country. You're really going to enjoy the smooth taste of this margarita, as the addition of Cointreau brings out the force of the agave nose in an excellent fresh-from-the-still 100-percent agave blanco tequila.

> 1 lemon or lime wedge
> Saucer of kosher salt (about ¼-inch deep)
> 1¼ ounces El Conquistador 100-percent blanco tequila
> 1 ounce Cointreau
> 1½ ounces freshly squeezed lemon or lime juice
> Ice

Run the lemon or lime wedge around the rim of a hurricane-style margarita glass. Dip the rim of the glass into the saucer of salt, rotating the rim in the salt until the desired amount has collected on the glass.

Measure the tequila, Cointreau, and lemon or lime juice into a 16-ounce cocktail shaker glass full of ice. Place a stainless steel cocktail shaker over the glass, tapping the top to create a seal. Shake vigorously for about 5 seconds and pour into the salt-rimmed glass.

Tequila Tidbit Tequila was imported legally for the first time into the United States during the late 1800s. During the Prohibition Era it was smuggled over the border from Mexico on a limited basis, but some say that because it was so easy to bring it over the border, Prohibition helped tequila to gain popularity in America.

Margarita Tip Maria's features a blue margarita, The Blue Angel, which uses blue triple sec that has been artificially colored. The strawberry margarita is red, and the peach is peach color, naturally. Why not try using food coloring in your margaritas for a special occasion—red, white, and blue for the Fourth of July, or red and green for Christmas?

THE GOLDEN GATE MARGARITA
Makes 1 margarita

This margarita is made with a new tequila called El Puente Viejo, "The Old Bridge." Even though the Golden Gate Bridge is not really that old, the grace of the lines and the golden beauty of it is well represented in this margarita. The golden hue that was imparted to this 100-percent agave tequila from its 90-day repose on oak is only surpassed by the wonderful flavor—a flavor full of agave with just a hint of spice. Mix it with Cointreau and lemon or lime juice and see why we are sold on the Golden Gate margarita.

1 lemon or lime wedge
Saucer of kosher salt (about ¼-inch deep)
1¼ ounces El Puente Viejo 100-percent agave reposado
    tequila
1 ounce Cointreau
1½ ounces freshly squeezed lemon or lime juice
Ice

Run the lemon or lime wedge around the rim of a hurricane-style margarita glass. Dip rim of the glass into the saucer of salt, rotating the rim in the salt until the desired amount has collected on the glass.

Measure the tequila, Cointreau, and lemon or lime juice into a 16-ounce cocktail shaker glass full of ice. Place a stainless steel cocktail shaker over the glass, tapping the top to create a seal. Shake vigorously for about 5 seconds and pour into the salt-rimmed glass.

Tequila Tidbit There are a few tequilas on the market in the United States that are priced over $200. One is Herradura Seleccion Supremas, a 100-percent agave tequila bottled in a limited-edition decanter and beautifully gift boxed. Another is Tres Cuatro Cinco (three, four, five), and it too is a 100-percent agave añejo tequila made from three different lots of tequila, one 3 years old, one 4 years old and one 5 years old. We do not use these two tequilas for margaritas because we would be paying mostly for the bottle, and since they are both limited editions, we could not keep up with the supply.

Margarita Tip Tequila is traced back as far as the late 1800s in the United States, but the margarita is a mere child. We estimate that the margarita was first invested just before or during World War II.

THE PUERTO VALLARTA MARGARITA
Makes 1 margarita

If you have kept the least bit informed about the huge growth of the boutique 100-percent agave tequila market, you would have joined us in saying, "Sooner or later someone was bound to name a tequila 'Puerto Vallarta.' " Here it is, and despite the predictable name, it is a great 100 percent agave reposado tequila at a very reasonable price. Puerto Vallarta comes in an attractive, but inexpensive bottle, and consequently we get a good value with this tequila. We mix it with Bols triple sec, so even more cost savings. The Puerto Vallarta Margarita is perhaps the best value of any margarita in this book.

> 1 lemon or lime wedge
> Saucer of kosher salt (about ¼-inch deep)
> 1¼ ounces Puerto Vallarta 100-percent agave reposado tequila
> 1 ounce Bols triple sec
> 1½ ounces freshly squeezed lemon or lime juice
> Ice

Run the lemon or lime wedge around the rim of a hurricane-style margarita glass. Dip the rim of the glass into the saucer of salt, rotating the rim in the salt until the desired amount has collected on the glass.

Measure the tequila, triple sec, and lemon or lime juice into a 16-ounce cocktail shaker glass full of ice. Place a stainless steel cocktail shaker over the glass, tapping the top to create a seal. Shake vigorously for about 5 seconds and pour into the salt-rimmed glass.

Tequila Tidbit Most agave growers trim the maturing plants to avoid workers stabbing themselves on the sharp ends of the leaves. Some tequila makers think that agave plants that are not trimmed during the growing period result in a stronger, healthier plant. The growers that don't trim their agave need very careful workers.

Margarita Tip If you can't find freshly squeezed lemon or lime juice and you don't want to bother with squeezing the lemons or limes yourself, be sure the juice you use in your margaritas is unsweetened. Beware of frozen "lemonades" or "limeades." They are generally packed with sugar. The best bet is still to squeeze your own.

LA MARGARITA DE ANFITRION

Makes 1 margarita

Another good value in a 100-percent agave reposado tequila: Anfitrion. Anfitrion means "host" in Spanish, so you may want to serve this margarita the next time you host an event at your home. You'll find that by mixing this fine 100-percent agave reposado tequila with Bols triple sec, you will not only have a wonderful cocktail, you will have one of the best bargains in a truly exquisite drink. Again, Anfitrion is packaged in a plain vanilla bottle, and the savings are passed on the consumer. You pay for the tequila, not the bottle. Serve this one the next time there's a big crowd coming over.

> 1 lemon or lime wedge
> Saucer of kosher salt (about ¼-inch deep)
> 1¼ ounces Anfitrion 100-percent agave reposado
>   tequila
> 1 ounce Bols triple sec
> 1½ ounces freshly squeezed lemon or lime juice
> Ice

Run the lemon or lime wedge around the rim of a hurricane-style margarita glass. Dip the rim of the glass into the saucer of salt, rotating the rim in the salt until the desired amount has collected on the glass.

Measure the tequila, triple sec, and lemon or lime juice into a 16-ounce cocktail shaker glass full of ice. Place a stainless steel cocktail shaker over the glass, tapping the top to create a seal. Shake vigorously for about 5 seconds and pour into the salt-rimmed glass.

Tequila Tidbit To convert the starch to sugar, the agave piña must be cooked. Most distillers will cook the agave in adobe or stone ovens called *hornos.* Most cook the agave for 48 hours and allow another 24 hours for cooling. After cooking, the agave turns dark brown and has a sweet taste. Other distilleries use large steel autoclaves to pressure-cook the agaves in only a few hours.

Margarita Tip Take particular care in washing your margarita shakers and glasses if you're using freshly squeezed juices. The pulp has a tendency to adhere to the surface of the utensil. Your best bet is to rinse the shaker and glasses as soon as possible after drinking the margarita, before the pulp has a chance to dry on the surface.

THE SOLDIER FROM SPAIN MARGARITA

Makes 1 margarita

Conquistador means "conqueror." Mexico was conquered, and New Mexico was settled by the conquistadors, or the soldiers of Spain. A lot of the history of tequila includes the conquistadors. It is they, for example, who decided that the pulque the Mexican Indians served them tasted so awful, they would improve the flavor by distilling it. And so tequila was born. It seems fitting that we now have a tequila named after these history makers, and even more so that we concoct a margarita that we can call "the Soldier from Spain."

> 1 lemon or lime wedge
> Saucer of kosher salt (about ¼-inch deep)
> 1¼ ounces El Conquistador 100-percent agave reposado tequila
> 1 ounce Cointreau
> 1½ ounces freshly squeezed lemon or lime juice
> Ice

Run the lemon or lime wedge around the rim of a hurricane-style margarita glass. Dip the rim of the glass into the saucer of salt, rotating the rim in the salt until the desired amount has collected on the glass.

Measure the tequila, Cointreau, and lemon or lime juice into a 16-ounce cocktail shaker glass full of ice. Place a stainless steel cocktail shaker over the glass, tapping the top to create a seal. Shake vigorously for about 5 seconds and pour into the salt-rimmed glass.

Tequila Tidbit The best selling tequila in 1997 was José Cuervo with almost half of all sales, 47 percent. Sauza is second with 13 percent; Montezuma, third with 11 percent; Juarez, 5 percent; and Pepe Lopez, 3 percent. All other brands, which include the superpremium, make up an outstanding 21 percent of the tequila market, which is all growth in the past 5 years.

Margarita Tip The key ingredient in a margarita is the tequila. The better the tequila, the better the margarita. But never skimp on the triple sec, and don't overwhelm the flavor of the tequila by using some commercial mix; squeeze your own lemons or limes if possible. Never use sugar.

EL GRAN CONQUISTADOR MARGARITA

Makes 1 margarita

If the other margaritas we've made from El Conquistador tequilas were wonderful, this one is grand. It uses the añejo-style tequila from this distiller and combines it with Grand Marnier. It is quite difficult to find a tequila that can challenge the flavor of Grand Marnier. If the tequilas not of good character and hearty flavor, with all of the agave goodness coming right to the front, one should not use it with Grand Marnier. Obviously, El Conquistador can stand up to Grand Marnier. And as a true margarita aficionado will tell you, there is no greater flavor than the combination of a great tequila and Grand Marnier.

1 lemon or lime wedge
Saucer of kosher salt (about ¼-inch deep)
1¼ ounces El Conquistador 100-percent agave añejo tequila
1 ounce Grand Marnier
1½ ounces freshly squeezed lemon or lime juice
Ice

Run the lemon or lime wedge around the rim of a hurricane-style margarita glass. Dip the rim of the glass into the saucer of salt, rotating the rim in the salt until the desired amount has collected on the glass.

Measure the tequila, Grand Marnier, and lemon or lime juice into a 16-ounce cocktail shaker glass full of ice. Place a stainless steel cocktail shaker over the glass, tapping the top to create a seal. Shake vigorously for about 5 seconds and pour into the salt-rimmed glass.

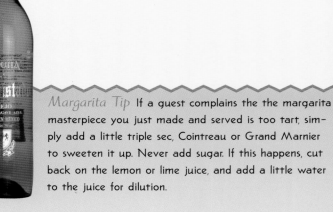

Margarita Tip If a guest complains the the margarita masterpiece you just made and served is too tart, simply add a little triple sec, Cointreau or Grand Marnier to sweeten it up. Never add sugar. If this happens, cut back on the lemon or lime juice, and add a little water to the juice for dilution.

CHAPTER FIVE

More Great Tequila Drinks

Tequila isn't just for margaritas. This chapter includes some bar favorites that use tequila but are not margaritas, as well as one "margarita" that doesn't use tequila.

THE STRAWBERRY MARGARITA
Makes 1 cocktail

This may not be a real margarita, but it sure as heck is a first cousin. Some of the most fun you can have with tequila (other than with margaritas) is the way you can mix it with fresh fruit and juices. As far as we're concerned, that's the only time a "frozen margarita" is justified. Let your imagination run wild when making fruit margaritas. The possibilities are almost endless—bananas, mangoes, papayas—but our favorites are margaritas made with strawberries and peaches (see page 115). Always use fresh fruit if you can, but if it's out of season, use unsweetened individually frozen fruits. We also recommend using simple syrup rather than the sugary citrus sweet-and-sour mix that most bars use in their so-called margaritas.

- 1¼ ounces José Cuervo Silver tequila
- 1 ounce Bols triple sec
- 1½ ounces freshly squeezed lemon juice
- 2 ounces simple syrup or sweet-and-sour mix
- 6 to 8 stemmed fresh or partially thawed frozen strawberries plus 1 fresh strawberry for garnish (optional)
- 2 cups cracked ice

Place all of the ingredients in a blender and blend until smooth. Pour the mixture into a hurricane-style margarita glass. For a garnish, cut a strawberry three-fourths up from its tip and place on the rim of the glass if you wish.

To Make Simple Syrup: Heat equal parts sugar and water to the boiling point. When the sugar has dissolved, remove from the heat and let cool. Keep in a capped bottle (does not need refrigeration).

THE PEACH MARGARITA
Makes 1 cocktail

Use the ripest, juiciest peaches you can find and slice them over the blender, so you don't waste a drop of the nectar. As with the preceding recipe, use unsweetened individually frozen peaches if the fresh fruit is out of season, but avoid sweetened frozen peaches as the drink will be too sweet. Be careful—these fruit cocktails are so delicious and flavorful that you tend to forget they contain alcohol.

- 1¼ ounces José Cuervo Silver tequila
- 1 ounce Bols triple sec
- 1½ ounces freshly squeezed lemon juice
- 2 ounces simple syrup (see page 138) or sweet-and-sour mix
- 1 peeled, pitted, and sliced fresh peach, or ¾-cup partially frozen peach slices
- 2 cups cracked ice

Place all of the ingredients in a blender and blend until smooth. Pour the mixture into a hurricane-style margarita glass.

THE CHIMAYÓ COCKTAIL
Makes 1 cocktail

Chimayó is an old village in a valley of the Sangre de Cristo mountains that was originally settled by the Spanish in the seventeenth century. It's located about 30 miles north of Santa Fe and remains a charming place that's well known for the healing properties of the holy dirt in the santuario (or church). Chimayó is also famous for its outstanding New Mexico red chiles, probably the best chiles in the world, as well as for its delicious red apples. The Jaramillo family invented this cocktail to promote the village and its apples, many of which are harvested in the orchards around its famous restaurant—the picturesque Rancho de Chimayó.

- Ice
- 1¼ ounces Herradura Silver tequila
- ¼ ounce crème de cassis
- 1 ounce fresh apple cider or juice
- ¼ ounce freshly squeezed lemon juice
- 1 red apple wedge

Fill a double old-fashioned glass with ice. Pour the tequila, crème de cassis, apple cider or juice, and lemon juice over the ice, and stir. Garnish the glass with an apple wedge and serve.

TEQUILA SUNRISE
Makes 1 cocktail

After the margarita, the Tequila Sunrise is perhaps the oldest and most popular tequila drink. As with all of these recipes, the better the ingredients, the better the final product. Use freshly squeezed juice and a good tequila; if ordering this at a bar or restaurant, be sure to avoid the house "well" brand, unless you know it's a premium tequila like Cuervo or Sauza (Cuervo Silver is the "well" brand at Maria's).

Ice
6 ounces freshly squeezed orange juice
1¼ ounces José Cuervo Silver tequila
Splash of grenadine
1 lime or orange wedge, or 1 maraschino cherry on a
    toothpick, for garnish (optional)

Fill a double old-fashioned glass three-quarters full of ice. Add the orange juice and tequila and stir. Add the grenadine. Garnish the glass with a fruit wedge or cherry, if desired, and serve.

THE LUCERO DE LA MAÑANA
Makes 1 cocktail

This is one of the most refreshing eye-openers you could imagine. The name of the cocktail is a pun on its creator's name (your humble author) and the Spanish translation is "morning star." It'll certainly be the star of your next breakfast or brunch party. Remember: the fresher and colder the orange juice, the better the drink.

Ice
1¼ ounces El Tesoro Plata tequila
8 ounces freshly squeezed orange juice
Splash of cranberry juice
1 lime or orange slice for garnish (optional)

Fill a 16-ounce tumbler with ice. Pour the tequila over the ice. Add the orange juice and stir. Add the cranberry juice and serve. If desired, garnish with a lime or orange slice.

THE GULF BREEZE
Makes 1 cocktail

This drink is the kissin' cousin of the previous cocktail. Same idea, different fruit juice. Remember, the colder the juice is, the better.

Ice
1¼ ounces El Tesoro Plata tequila
8 ounces freshly squeezed grapefruit juice
Splash of cranberry juice
1 lime or orange slice for garnish (optional)

Fill a 16-ounce tumbler with ice. Pour the tequila over the ice. Add the grapefruit juice and stir. Add the cranberry juice and serve. If desired, garnish with a lime or orange slice.

THE BLOODY MARIA
Makes 1 cocktail

Look again! Yes, it's Bloody Maria rather than Mary, and if you've already figured out that we use tequila rather than vodka, go to the head of the bartending class! Be sure to follow our recipe exactly, and more than likely you'll agree it's the best Bloody Maria or Mary you've ever had.

Ice
1 ounce José Cuervo Silver tequila
2 lime wedges (each ⅛ of a lime)
1 quick shot Worcestershire sauce
7 dashes Tabasco sauce
Salt and black pepper to taste
1 cup tomato juice (preferably Sacramento brand)

Fill a 16-ounce tumbler three-quarters full of ice. Pour the tequila over the ice. Squeeze one of the lime wedges into the glass. Add the Worcestershire sauce and the Tabasco (use less if you prefer) and shake a generous amount of salt and pepper into the glass. Fill the glass with tomato juice and stir vigorously. Float the juice from the second squeezed lime wedge over the top of the mixture. Run the squeezed lime wedge around the rim of the glass and drop it into the mixture. Do not stir again.

Sprinkle more salt and pepper on top of the mixture and on the rim of the glass so that a little sticks, then serve.

THE ABSOLUT MARGARITA
Makes 1 cocktail

We all know people who insist that they're allergic to whatever it is they don't like (or don't want to try). One regular customer at Maria's would watch us experimenting with margaritas, but when we offered to let her try a sip, she claimed to be allergic to tequila. So we came up with this cocktail for our customer so she could drink margaritas without drinking tequila. This may not be a "real" margarita, but you'll still enjoy it.

> 1 lemon or lime wedge
> Sauce of kosher salt (about ¼-inch deep)
> 1¼ ounces Absolut vodka
> 1 ounce Cointreau
> 1½ ounces freshly squeezed lemon or lime juice
> Ice

Run the lemon or lime wedge around the rim of a hurricane-style margarita glass. Dip the rim of the glass into the saucer of salt, rotating the rim in the salt until the desired amount has collected on the glass.

Measure the vodka, Cointreau, and lemon or lime juice into a 16-ounce cocktail shaker glass full of ice. Place a stainless steel cocktail shaker over the glass, tapping the top to create a seal. Shake vigorously for about 5 seconds and pour into the salt-rimmed glass.

CHAPTER SIX

MARIA'S NEW MEXICAN KITCHEN
Food to Serve with Margaritas

If you're going to the trouble of making margaritas with some of the wonderful tequilas we've described earlier, you may as well go whole hog and rustle up some New Mexican classics for the table. Somehow, the two go together perfectly, as we've discovered at Maria's. The recipes that follow are simple, straightforward, and truly represent the Southwestern cuisine of Old Santa Fe.

Note: All ingredients listed in these recipes are assumed to be of medium size, unless otherwise stated. For most of the typical New Mexican–grown ingredients, see "Resources" (page 150) for mail-order availability.

GUACAMOLE

Makes about 6 cups

Some things were made to go together. Guacamole, corn tortilla chips, and margaritas, for example, have a natural affinity. We believe that guacamole, like margaritas, must be made by hand. The other secret of great guacamole is to use the ripest Haas avocados you can find; they're the wrinkly ones with the deep, dark, purplish-green color. This recipe will create a dip that's guaranteed to go fast and avoid leftovers!

6 ripe Haas avocados, peeled and pitted
½-cup seeded and chopped New Mexico green chiles
1 yellow onion, finely chopped
1 ripe firm tomato, finely diced
4 garlic cloves, minced
Dash of Worcestershire sauce
Juice of ½ lemon
Salt to taste
Tortilla chips

In a large stainless steel or ceramic bowl, mash the pitted avocado with a fork, leaving chunks no larger than half an inch across. Add the green chiles, onion, tomato, and garlic, and blend together. Blend in the Worcestershire sauce and lemon juice (being careful to strain any seeds). Add the salt and serve with corn tortilla chips.

If not serving immediately, place an avocado pit in the center of the dip, cover the bowl with plastic wrap, and refrigerate. This will minimize the oxidation that turns the surface of the guacamole brown.

NEW MEXICO FAMILY-STYLE TACOS

Serves 6 (makes 12 tacos)

This simple recipe can be halved, doubled, tripled, or whatever. The recipe was designed for soft tacos (kept warm by covering them with a cloth), but the crisp U-shaped taco shells are a treat, as well. You can add a bowl of sour cream, guacamole, or different taco sauces or salsas according to your fancy.

1 pound extra-lean ground beef
Vegetable oil for frying
12 yellow or blue corn tortillas
1 yellow onion, coarsely chopped
2 ripe tomatoes, coarsely chopped
2 cups (8 ounces) shredded Cheddar cheese
½ head iceberg lettuce, coarsely chopped
Maria's World-Famous Salsa (see page 147) or your
    favorite taco sauce or salsa
Salt and pepper to taste

In a large skillet or sauté pan, sauté the ground beef until cooked through and browned. Drain off fat and place the beef in a large serving bowl.

In another skillet or sauté pan, heat about ½ inch of vegetable oil until very hot. Fry a tortilla for 5 to 10 seconds, or just until softened, holding it with cooking tongs. Do not allow the tortilla to become crisp.

Place the tortilla on a paper towel on a serving plate and repeat until all the tortillas are fried, layering paper towels between them to absorb the oil. If not serving immediately, cover the tortillas with a clean dish towel to keep warm.

Place the onion, tomatoes, cheese, lettuce, and salsa or taco sauce in separate serving bowls in the center of the table along with the meat and tortillas. Place a tortilla on a serving plate, spoon some beef in the center of the tortilla, add salsa or taco sauce, salt, and pepper, then sprinkle a little onion, tomato, cheese, and lettuce on top of the beef (in that order). Fold the tortilla to form a soft taco, pick it up, and eat.

MARIA'S BLUE CORN ENCHILADAS

Makes 4 servings

Grind your own dried New Mexico red chiles or use pure New Mexico red chile powder for this recipe. Any other chile powder is just not the same. To make a vegetarian chile sauce, just eliminate the ground beef.

Red Chile Enchilada Sauce:

2 tablespoons vegetable shortening or lard
9 heaping tablespoons New Mexico red chile powder
4 quarts cold water
1 heaping tablespoon all-purpose flour
4 garlic cloves, minced
1 teaspoon salt
2 pounds extra-lean ground beef

Enchiladas:

Vegetable oil for frying
12 blue, yellow, or white corn tortillas
2 cups coarsely chopped onions
2 cups coarsely chopped tomatoes
4 cups (1 pound) shredded Cheddar cheese
½ head iceberg lettuce, shredded

To prepare the Red Chile Enchilada Sauce, melt the shortening or lard in a large saucepan over medium-high heat until just smoking. Add the chile powder, 1 tablespoon at a time, whisking constantly to avoid lumping. When too thick to whisk, add ½ cup of the water. Heat a little and continue to add the chile powder, alternating with the water, until all the water and all the chile powder have been combined.

In a small bowl, mix the flour with a little water until the flour is dissolved. Add this flour-water mixture to the chile powder mixture and bring to a light boil. Stir in the garlic and salt. Set aside and keep warm.

Sauté the ground beef in a large skillet or sauté pan until medium-rare. Drain off the fat and add the ground beef to the enchilada sauce. Cook for 45 minutes to 1 hour, stirring occasionally.

Preheat the oven to 200°F.

To prepare the enchiladas, heat about ½ inch of vegetable oil in a medium skillet until very hot. Fry one tortilla at a time for 5 to 10 seconds, or just until softened. Do not allow the tortillas to become crisp. Drain excess the oil by holding the tortillas with tongs over the pan.

Drop one tortilla into the Red Chile Enchilada Sauce to saturate, then place it flat on a deep individual ovenproof plate or dish. Sprinkle some of the onions, tomatoes, and cheese over the tortilla, and top with an additional ¼ cup of the enchilada sauce. Saturate a second tortilla in Red Chile Enchilada Sauce and place it over the first. Top with onions, tomatoes, and cheese and another ¼ cup of the enchilada sauce.

Top with a third tortilla (the tortillas will look like a stack of pancakes covered with red chile sauce). Spoon the enchilada sauce over the top of the stack and sprinkle with cheese.

Place the tortilla stack in the preheated oven. Repeat the process for 3 more serving plates or dishes. Serve at once, garnished with the lettuce and remaining chopped tomatoes, and accompanied with your favorite margarita.

MARIA'S WORLD-FAMOUS SALSA
Makes about 3 cups

This is a great taco sauce for the preceding recipe, and it is ideal as a dip with corn tortilla chips.

  2 cups chunky tomato sauce
  1 cup seeded and chopped New Mexico green chiles
  ½ cup water
  ½ teaspoon salt
  1 tablespoon minced garlic
  ¼ cup diced yellow onion
  2 tablespoons crushed red chile flakes or chile powder

Combine all the ingredients well in a mixing bowl and adjust seasonings to taste. Cover and chill. Keep refrigerated for up to 3 days.

MARIA'S FRIJOLES

Makes about 8 cups

This bean recipe is so easy, so inexpensive, and so delicious that it should become a staple in anyone's repertoire of Southwestern food. It's also the perfect base for refried beans (see below). Use only pinto beans for this recipe, and ask for "new crop" if you have a choice. Never leave a pot of beans to cook while you leave the house; they could go dry and burn (it's happened).

> **1 pound dried pinto beans**
> **4 quarts water**
> **6 ounces salt pork, cut into ½-inch cubes**

Thoroughly sort through the beans to remove any foreign objects such as stones or twigs. Rinse the beans under cold water and place in a large (at least 8-quart) stew pot covered with the water. Soak for 1 to 2 hours, or overnight.

Add the salt pork to the beans and soaking water and bring to a rolling boil. Reduce the heat and simmer, uncovered, for at least 2 hours, or until tender enough to mash. Add more water if at any time the beans are covered by less than 2 inches. Stir from time to time to make sure the beans are not sticking to the bottom of the pot. The longer the beans cook, the better they will taste.

For Vegetarian Frijoles: Replace the salt pork with 2 tablespoons of vegetable shortening and add salt during the last 30 minutes of cooking (adding salt earlier will make the beans tough).

For Refried Beans: Mash the drained, cooked beans with a fork and simmer in hot bacon fat or vegetable oil for about 10 minutes, stirring constantly.

AL'S CHEDDAR CHEESE AND ONION BEAN DIP

Makes about 8 cups

Here's a great bean dip that uses ingredients that are available just about anywhere. It's easy to make and virtually foolproof, but it does require some time and effort to prepare, as well as a chafing dish, fondue dish, or some kind of heated serving apparatus to keep the dip warm (a crockpot at its lowest setting would also work). You can make a smaller amount of the dip by dividing the recipe in half.

> 1 tablespoon solid vegetable shortening
> 4 cups drained Maria's Frijoles (see page 148) (reserve the broth)
> 1 large onion, diced
> 3 garlic cloves, finely minced
> 1 cup Maria's World-Famous Salsa (see page 147) or other picante tomato-based salsa
> 1 cup seeded and chopped New Mexico green chiles
> 4 cups (1 pound) shredded Cheddar cheese
> Tortilla chips

In a large skillet or sauté pan, melt the shortening over medium-high heat. Add the beans and mash them while frying. Lower the heat and continue to fry mashed beans until heated through.

Transfer beans to a larger saucepan, adding the onion, garlic, salsa, and green chiles. Cook over medium heat, stirring constantly. Slowly add the cheese, stirring to blend (if the mixture becomes too thick, add a little of the reserved bean broth). Once the mixture is blended smoothly, transfer to a chafing dish, fondue dish, or crockpot. Serve with tortilla chips.

RESOURCES

Following is a list of importers and/or distributors of tequilas and other products called for in the recipes throughout Maria's. If you can't find one of the tequilas or other products mentioned in this book at your local grocery or liquor store, simply call, write, or fax one of the sources listed below and ask for the nearest dealer.

Please bear in mind that, as in all industries, changes in the tequila industry occur constantly. While it is our intent to provide you with the most current, up-to-date source list, the following information is subject to change.

Centinela
Eldorado Importers
761 Parker Ave.
Santa Rose, New Mexico 88435
(800) 468-0672

Cointreau
Rémy American, Inc.
Cointreau Division
1350 Avenue of the Americas,
7th Floor
New York, New York 10019
(212) 399-4200

El Tesoro
Robert Denton & Co.
2724 Auburn Rd.
Auburn Hills, Michigan 48326
(800) 669-7808
Fax: (313) 299-3836

El Viejito
Paterno Imports
4242 N. Capistrano, Unit No. 128
Dallas, Texas 75287
(214) 733-0340
Fax: (214) 733-0072

Paterno Imports
2701 S. Western Ave.
Chicago, Illinois 60608
(312) 247-7070

Grand Marnier
Carillon Importers, Ltd.
Glenpointe Center West
Teaneck, New Jersey 07666
(201) 836-7799

Herradura
Sazerac Co., Inc.
P.O. Box 52821
New Orleans, Louisiana 70152-2821
(504) 831-2323
Fax: (504) 831-2323

Hussong's
McCormick Distilling Co.
1 McCormick Lane
Weston, Missouri 64098
(816) 640-2276

Hussong's
Cantina SAA de CV
Ave Ruiz No. 113
Encenada, Mexico BC22800

José Cuervo
José Cuervo International, Inc.
25950 Acero, Suite 250
Mission Viejo, California 92691
(714) 583-7755

Patrón
St. Maarten Spirits, Ltd.
8460 Higuera
Culver City, California 90232
(800) 723-4767
Fax: (310) 841-2335

Sauza
Domecq Importers, Inc.
143 Sound Beach Ave.
Old Greenwich, Connecticut 06870
(800) 697-6547
Fax: (203) 637-6595

Margarita Glasses
Libbey Glass, Inc.
940 Ash St.
Toledo, Ohio 43693
(419) 729-7272

New Mexican Cooking Ingredients
Bueno Foods
2001 4th St. SW
Albuquerque, New Mexico 87102
(800) 95-CHILE

INDEX